To read *Mourning and Milestones* is to experience whole-hearted living. When one encounters profound loss there is an equal measure of grace that appears as a blessed surprise. Kathleen shows us how to stay present—awake, alive, alert, fully conscious—especially when it hurts.

Everyone talks about being present, but who can bear it? Especially, when there is overwhelming loss and grief? To let our hearts be broken open again and again is a task no one signs up for. It hurts.

And yet, Kathleen shows us how it's done. She courageously meets *this* moment, *this* situation, *this* unexpected turn with eyes and heart open, refusing to let her loss diminish her connection to family, self or, her beloved Jack. Her writing is passionate, practical, articulate, and illuminating.

Leah Ruekberg, writer, producer of Stories Roc! and instructor at the Writers and Books Literary Center

This is a beautifully written, brave and honest book about loss. In eploring the special "milestone" days, Kathleen Fraser creates a roadmap to help surviving spouses navigate their conflicted feelings and needs in the months and first years after a loss. Birthdays, anniversaries and holidays can trigger unfinished grief and can overwhelm many mourners. Kathleen is able to show so clearly how this affects not just the spouse, but the whole family. Her simple but detailed, concrete "hints" can "ease the burden of invention" families face, whether creating new traditions, ceremonies or even in the process of scattering ashes. Those who grieve will also appreciate the courage she finds to tackle the trauma of sudden loss in our modern world and how critical it is to share those emotions with someone safe. Kathleen has experienced the challenging balance between "honoring loss" and living in the present, between wanting support from others and needing to be alone, between acknowledging the hard pain and seeking out her own joy and strengths. I look forward to sharing the many comforting passages in this valuable book with anyone who is grieving.

Arlene Levitt, counselor, educator, and bereavement group facilitator

In twenty-five years of professional ministry, I have waited for a resource like this. Dr. Fraser's personal account provides a sensitive, compassionate yet unvarnished roadmap for those times when the grief process can seem overwhelming and without direction. Not only perfect for professionals, this book provides hope for all who have survived the death of a loved one. A great read: compassionate, loving, humorous . . . honest!

The Reverend Deborah Fae Swift
South Presbyterian Church

Kathleen Fraser captures the essence of the varied experiences of losing one's spouse. *Mourning and Milestones* shows the slow process of building a new life and reveals some of the most intimate details of her life with Jack. I was both riveted by Fraser's story and drawn to reflecting on my own experience. Her accounts of other widows/widowers and the additional resources section add dimension to her own story.

Stephen L. Fielding, Ph.D.

In these pages, Kathleen Fraser shows us the very human reality of her agonizing personal experience in the days, weeks, months, and years following the sudden death of her beloved husband, allowing us a vivid glimpse into the everyday moments that make up the lived experience of grief. In a narrative beautifully crafted with mindfulness and tenderness, this book explores the ways that milestones, anniversaries, trigger points, and even seemingly innocuous daily events can catapult a grieving person into the chaos of emotions that make up the experience of loss. Fraser's story will resonate with anyone who has been through the trials of grief, loss, or transformation. For anyone traveling the road of grief and mourning, this book would be a treasured companion on the journey."

Shira May, communication coach, adjunct instructor
of speech communication at Monroe Community College

MOURNING *and* MILESTONES

Honoring
Anniversaries,
Birthdays, and
Special Occasions
After a Loved
One Dies

KATHLEEN FRASER

**TURNING
STONE
PRESS**

Cover design by Frame25 Productions
Cover art by ilolab c/o Shutterstock.com
Interior design by Jane Hagaman

Turning Stone Press
8301 Broadway, Suite 219
San Antonio, TX 78209
www.turningstonepress.com

Library of Congress Cataloging-in-Publication Data available upon
request.

ISBN 978-1-61852-102-6

10 9 8 7 6 5 4 3 2 1

Printed in the United States of America

Contents

Part One: My Journey

Part Two: Others' Journeys

To Jack

We loved each other passionately, fiercely, quietly, deeply, playfully, as lovers, friends, parents, grandparents, and as searchers of the secret depths of the heart and soul. Then you died. Gone was the scent of the outdoors you carried inside when you worked in the yard, the taste of the soups you made on Saturdays using the art of free substitution, the sound of you coming home from work, our touches as we worked together, your blue eyes so full of life, the comfort of your presence, access to your wisdom, and the way we always had each other's backs. Our vows said until death do us part. Yet the love remains and you remain and death is not a final parting.

You are there in the teenage grandsons who retain a sweetness and gentleness of spirit. They seem to know that it lies close to the core of being a man. You are there in the confidence, self-assurance, and creativity of our granddaughters. You are there in the lives of your children, who choose to walk ethically and socially responsible paths. In them, there is a little of your walk, your face, your laugh, and your vitality.

You adopted my children, and your love and commitment to them live on. I see you in their strength, their appreciation of gardens and presentation of food, their memories, their continuation of the things you did together, and in the health you helped them achieve.

You live in our love that did not die. You live in the way I nurture parts of me that reflect parts of you. You knew what mattered and what did not. You gardened with love, found the good in those you met, gave no energy to judging others, welcomed adventure, taught me the importance of celebration, and sought purpose and opportunities to be of service. You live on in the business ventures you coaxed into being, the people you inspired, the home you repaired, and the gardens you designed and tended.

You live on in me. I am forever changed by being loved so well and by having my love welcomed so deeply. I am still growing into the person you loved, and I am sustained by the memory of the self I saw reflected in your eyes.

Foreword

It's my great pleasure to write a forward in response to *Mourning and Milestones.*

Kathleen Fraser writes sensitively and wisely from her own experiences and her interviews with others who have been in her shoes. Kathleen was an articulate and caring member of a support group at Lifetime Care. Members and facilitators both treasured her input and her loving listening to her cohort of grieving men and women. As she showed her own mastery of a devastating loss, she went on to assist others to approach their own tragedies through expressive writing and deep delving.

Mourning and Milestones is a result of her own grief work, well done. The book fills an important niche for bereaved men and women suffering major loss as they face social pressures of holiday seasons, as well as special days that are more personal and intimate. Readers will immediately relate to the text and practical suggestions; they will also appreciate the supportive tone conveyed throughout.

This is really a support group in the form of a book! I believe it will be welcomed as an oasis in the midst of the isolation and desert storms that follow major loss. Supportive friends, neighbors, and colleagues who wish to help would also benefit from the information and creative approaches to minimizing pain.

Our world would be a more compassionate place for mourners if this book were widely read.

—Theo Munson, Community Bereavement Services
at Lifetime Care in Rochester, NY

Introduction

In 1989, I moved to Rochester, New York. One day after we moved, my children were in an auto accident with their father, who died in the crash. My children, Erica (age eight) and Greg (age eleven), were injured but recovered fully. Learning to get through this time taught me something about survival after loss and let me know that we all have the strength to do it.

Moving left us without a community, but we found one at a local parish. Church had not always been a natural home for us, but we found this one open and welcoming. Its natural spirit of inquiry and acceptance resonated with us. A few years after joining, I met Jack there. He noticed me singing in the choir, and I noticed his gentle friendly face watching us sing. His spirit of openness, intellectual curiosity, ethical grounding, strong sense of the importance of family, blue eyes, and broad shoulders drew me in. We spoke after the service and both became very regular attendees after we met. As a widower, Jack knew a lot about loss and raising children on your own.

Dating too soon after our first marriages had led each of us to some regrettable relationship choices. We were cautious this time. We both felt that the other was someone very special we wanted to keep in our lives. So we continued to meet after services.

Jack told me that his head was turned for sure when I bought the Christmas tree for the church and just showed up with it. My turning point was when we loaded the dishwasher together after the Christmas party, and it became a pleasant chore. He knew how to move easily and cooperatively in tight spaces. He came to see me play bass at a benefit concert and mentioned this as another key moment.

We started doing things together as friends, denying that there might be more for many months. His children were grown, but mine were at home. That added importance to the care we took to be sure how we felt before entering into a romance. My children put Jack through many tests, but as a seasoned parental pro, he saw the tests for what they were and knew how to respond.

Jack told me often that he was drawn to my competence and independence, as I was to his. We each trusted that the other knew something important from having had a spouse die and raising children who had lost a parent. When we met, I was a college professor in a male-dominated field, an active musician, a homeowner who could do her own repairs, and a single parent. Within a year of our marriage, I became ill with CFS/ME (Chronic Fatigue Syndrome/

Myalgic Encephalomyelitis). Over the next many years, as my health declined, I switched from teaching to a desk job, from the desk job to teaching online, eventually becoming too disabled to hold a job.

Jack's love never wavered. I had trouble knowing who I was without a profession, but he always knew who I was. He appreciated whatever I was able to do and brought the outside world home to me when I was too ill to be out in it myself. He helped me teach when I tried to continue working. He pushed the wheelchair so that I could travel. He supported me when I embarked on a search for experimental treatments. He was always there for me, remained proud that I was his wife, and let others know how much he loved me.

We loved each other first as individuals, then our love deepened as we grew to be parents together. He was a father to my children and loved them as the individuals they are. He was a man who accepted people as they were and found places to connect and relate. He taught me about all-encompassing love and a way of depending on each other without losing individuality. I watched him grow as a grandparent, finding new depth in our love from the joy of being grandparents together.

We were married for almost eighteen romantic years. Most of those years included caring for children or grandchildren, his dad, and then my dad. So we took advantage of little moments. Cooking or cleaning up would be time for a gentle touch or embrace. A trip to the grocery store became a date. Going to the hardware store was an opportunity for nesting.

Jack died of a heart attack at home on March 7, 2011. The month before he died, in gratitude for my work homeschooling our grandson, he declared all of February Valentine's Day. We went to concerts and movies and took walks on the winter beach. The Sunday before he died, he found a moment to tell me from the depth of his heart that he loved me. We often said those words, but on that day, he said it with a strength and conviction that will stay with me forever.

Jack's death was sudden, shocking, and unexpected. His doctor and all who knew him saw him as vibrantly alive and youthful. When he died, our family included my adult son and daughter, her husband, Jack's three adult children, two daughters-in-law, and five grandchildren.

As we mourn his loss and struggle to continue with our lives without him, we face major challenges on the days that carry special meaning: holidays, anniversaries, or birthdays. Each time one of these milestone dates approaches, there is a sense of unease, anxiety, or unmooring. The quality and strength of the discomfort may vary, but it always comes. Usually a sense of disorientation or an increased difficulty in managing slowly builds on its own. Then one of us remembers that an anniversary or special day is coming.

Each time the anniversary of Jack's death approaches, I experience an ominous foreboding that something awful is about to happen. It makes no sense, but it is real. As Christmas nears, I find myself dreading the day, afraid of how I will get through it and wishing it could be completely ignored.

Yet, as a mother and a grandmother, this is not a choice I feel I can make.

We struggle as individuals and as a family to find ways to celebrate Jack's presence in our lives. We work to balance giving respect to mourning his loss and honoring our determination to live the lives we have. We search for the secret trick to meeting our own needs, supporting one another, sharing our grief and our joy, and leaving space for burying our heads in the blankets. We stumble toward approaches that include trying to figure out what might work for us, planning a strategy for how to manage the day, and leaving room for responses and needs we cannot anticipate. The exhaustion and confusion of grief make finding creative ways to honor Jack's life and our love for him especially challenging. It is tough to invent this stuff on our own.

In this book, I'll share my experiences with the milestone days, one ordinary day, ideas I've collected from other bereaved spouses, and some ideas that were shared in grief support groups. The series of essays in parts 1 and 2 include a few thoughts that emerged as I contemplated the ups and downs, fits and starts, surprises, sidesteps, and confusion of grieving. The appendix provides some specific ideas you might wish to borrow.

It is my hope that having examples of what others have done might lighten your load as you search for your own ways to make it through the landmark days. I hope to ease the burden of invention with information and perhaps support your decisions to make these days what you need them to be.

Part One

My Journey

Chapter One

The First Year

The First Milestones/Jubilee Week I

About two months after the death of my husband, Jack, our family hit its first major milestone. Jack used to call the week in mid-May—which includes Mother's Day, our anniversary, and his birthday—Jubilee Week. He would always take time off from work to celebrate and would often plan a trip or excursions. Jubilee Week came up very quickly after his death. I knew I would need the support of family and to get out of town to make it through.

I was the homeschool instructor for my thirteen-year-old grandson, Devlin, who was living with me from Monday to Friday. He was there when Jack collapsed, when the emergency crew arrived, and when we learned in the hospital that there was nothing they could do. I had to find a way to care for myself on those difficult days and deeply wished to include Devlin. I did not know if I would be able to provide any love and support, but I struggled to find a plan that would create the space we needed without overwhelming us. It was clear that I could not do this in our home. It was full of reminders of Jack's collapse, loving memories of celebrations of his birth, and the joy I took in his life and our marriage.

My family, including Devlin, is fascinated by the ocean, finds pleasure being in it and peace staring at it. My sister, Jean, brother-in-law, Dan, and niece Anna—all of whom love Devlin—lived in Sarasota, Florida, near the ocean. So I asked them if Devlin, my daughter, Erica, and I could visit in May. They found us a place to stay in the RV park where Dan worked. They agreed to arrange an adventure with Devlin on my anniversary day so that I would not have to think about his care. They gave me the gift of space to quietly let the day take me wherever it led. My daughter stayed with me for support, and it was needed.

Wedding Anniversary

I don't remember much about that first anniversary day. I know that it included talking about my marriage, being together, sharing how much we missed Jack, and healing time in the water. Jean, Dan, and Devlin had a full day of adventure and fun. Then Devlin rejoined Erica and me at the end of the day in the RV park pool. For the anniversary, I needed quiet, contemplative solo time and the space to not have to try to hold it together. But for the birthday, it seemed important to include everyone.

Jack's Birthday

On Jack's birthday, we all agreed to meet in the evening at Anna's house for a small ceremony of remembrance. During the day, we spent time at the ocean, swimming and gazing out at the horizon. There were enough of us around to keep the things a bit light, but still it was a painful day. When evening came, we gathered around the fire pit near the shore of a large pond in Anna's backyard and sat chatting for an hour or so. Devlin built a fire log by log and slowly a sense of camaraderie and companionship grew as we sat around the blaze. The fire gave us space to chat or just sit quietly. At times, it was mesmerizing. Its beauty helped us move from the routines of daily life to a different, more ceremonial space.

As our sense of quiet deepened, I asked everyone to write a letter to Jack, saying whatever needed to be said. I suggested the letter could be about how they were missing him, their love for him, his love for them, or just what they wished to share about the last couple of months. Each person wrote and wrote while quiet tears were shed. Words just seemed to flow from our pens. When we were all done, we burned our missives, sending them out in the rising smoke and ash to our beloved husband, father, grandfather, uncle, and brother-in-law. No one read their letter aloud, but we did talk about writing and what we said. We sat by the fire a while longer, until we were ready to return to ordinary time. It felt as if we had done just the right thing to honor Jack and our own grief. It was enough and not too much.

Making this plan was more difficult than its simplicity makes it seem. I tried to talk with others about making a plan, but for the most part, it was up to me. I don't know if their resistance reflected the difficulty of confronting pain or respect for my loss and a sense that my grief came first. I learned later that it was very hard for people to participate in this ritual. Afterward, there was tangible relief that we had made it through, and everyone was glad they had participated.

For me, there was really no choice. I needed a framework for the grief of the day, a place to put it, a way to combat the fear that the grief would just engulf me. Family members who had not participated in Jack's birthday celebrations over the years could have let the day slip by unnoticed. My gratitude for the choice they made to be with me will be part of me for a long time.

Thoughts

♦ **Sometimes, when a milestone brings up devastating grief, it can help to get away.**

♦ **Those who love you may need you to tell them what you need.**

♦ **Children may need to grieve in their own way.**

♦ **Enlist help.**

♦ **Try writing a letter to your loved one.**

Father's Day I

Our first Father's Day without Jack came a little more than three months after his death. My daughter, Erica, my son,

Greg, and my son-in-law, Dean, were all at my home, and we needed to be together. My memories of these early months are cloudy, but there are parts of the day that stand out for me. Father's Day can be a difficult holiday for us. Greg and Erica's biological dad died when they were eleven and eight, respectively. He suffered from recurring extreme depression and other psychological and physical issues. At best, he was an indifferent but interesting father; at worst, an abusive one. His death brought a mixture of grief and relief.

Jack was a chosen father. Shortly after we were married, Jack adopted Greg and Erica, and we began the slow process of building a two-parent family. Over time, his relationships with the two of them grew out of love, respect, shared interests, shared adventures, and conversations over dinner. For Erica, there were also late-night snacks that coincided with Jack's early breakfasts.

At Jack's memorial service, Greg spoke about how Jack had chosen all of us when he married me. In fact, we all chose him, a man who was a father who celebrated my children's accomplishments and chose to know them deeply as individuals. Of course, there were struggles. But Jack had raised three teens. His quiet, balanced view of what mattered and what did not gave him a grace and credibility that formed a basis for the mature love the three of them shared. Dean had been developing his own relationship of affection and respect with Jack and felt the loss of the future they had looked forward to together.

Father's Day knocked all of us down with a sharp, acute grief filled with thoughts of the important milestones to come that would not include Jack's physical presence. There are children who will be born who will not know him as a grandfather, graduate school graduations he will not celebrate, Greg's eventual marriage at which Jack will not give a toast. We mourned in advance all of the occasions during which Jack's presence or advice or listening ear would be missed. He was fun, interesting, loving, and eager to learn about the things each of us was learning and doing. Also, he was the only one who knew what glasses to serve with which beverages.

We were very lucky that the four of us could be together. After Jack's death, Greg, Erica, and I feared that we would revert to the tight trio we had formed after their biological dad's death. We were aware that this would not serve us well now. Making space for Dean and others who were in our lives or might come into our lives was essential. Dean's physical presence and his quiet help throughout the day joined us in our shared grief. There were meals and conversations about Jack that helped, but I cannot remember the specifics. Our primary way of celebrating Jack was to engage in a springtime ritual that he had often led.

There is a small pond in our backyard that is just big enough for fish to overwinter if the neighborhood cats don't fish them out. So, when grandchildren or a great-niece visited, Jack engaged them in helping him restock the pond. Sometimes, he just took them to the pet store for goldfish, but the best stocking trips were adventures with nets, jars, and buckets to Mendon Ponds Park. Catching very small fish in nets and jars is a pretty great activity. It takes a long time, because it is challenging, it is quiet and beautiful in the woods, and messing around in a pond gets you satisfyingly muddy.

Unfortunately, all of the usual collection gear seemed to have disappeared. So the four of us went to the park armed with various potentially useful items found around the kitchen. We located a quiet spot with easy access to Jack's favorite pond and set about trying to capture a few of the small fish that were darting all around us. The fish showed much more skill in eluding us than we demonstrated in catching them. Luckily, a young boy with a fishing rod and precision fishing skills came along and offered his assistance. Of course, we agreed because we needed the help and because, without question, Jack would have included this child in the endeavor.

We spent a couple of hours in the park wading around, looking for good spots, and fishing in the pond. Making fools of ourselves missing fish after fish lightened the day, giving us chances for easy connections. The young stranger caught all of the fish that we brought home, and some made it through this last winter.

We hold an intention to incorporate gratitude for Jack's life and what he gave us into our lives and rituals or celebrations. But it can feel forced when the overpowering feeling is loss. Our young fisherman's persistence in helping us achieve

Thoughts

- Try to engage in an activity that evokes your loved one's spirit or playful side.

- Leave space for serendipity.

- Sharing grief can help.

- A good ritual can include a willingness to seem foolish.

- Mourning can include anticipation of future events without your loved one.

our goal, and our awareness that caring for Jack created this opportunity, made a natural opening for gratitude to slip in and soften our grief.

Thanksgiving I

In 2010, approximately five months before Jack's death in March 2011, Thanksgiving was at my house; family from out of town stayed in our extra bedrooms. They brought favorite foods and collaborated to make a feast that would feed all sixteen of us into stupors. Jack and my brother-in-law Jeff had a grand time working together on the turkey, and the kitchen was full from morning until dinnertime with chefs creating the dishes that their nuclear families could not do without. When Jack and Jeff finished their turkey preparation, they gleefully retreated, good beer in hand, to enjoy the ritual of watching the football game while the turkey roasted.

Thanksgiving 2011 did not hold the same promise. The name of the holiday specifies an attitude of gratitude, but my primary emotion approaching the holiday was a pervasive weariness and some dread. Being part of a large family, a multiday gathering seemed overwhelming.

Greg and Erica were in Rochester with me. My stepdaughter, Elizabeth, and her son, Devlin, live nearby. Devlin was living with me during the week for homeschooling, but he was with his mom for the holiday. There is a great deal of stress between our homes that has only amplified since Jack's death. Our challenge was how to get through the day without rubbing in how hard it was without Jack. He always played a big role in the preparations and provided the glue that made this group a family.

It took days of thought to come up with a plan, but for the first time in my memory, I did not work hard to make sure that Thanksgiving was a success for my extended family. It was worth the preparation, because we ended up with a nice holiday together. Prior to Thanksgiving Day, I made it known that I was not up to preparing the traditional meal for everyone. Elizabeth and Devlin planned a turkey dinner for themselves with their next-door neighbor. Erica made evening plans with local friends, and Greg and I planned to attend an evening Thanksgiving dinner with a group of adults who create family out of friendships.

As the day neared, I began to see just how important it was for Devlin that I find a way of acknowledging we were all still a family who could celebrate together. Luckily, I saw an ad for a lunchtime Thanksgiving feast at a favorite Indian restaurant. This worked for us. Elizabeth was glad for the invitation, and the five of us met in a good way for a meal on a day meant for feasting with family.

The food was dramatically different from a traditional Thanksgiving dinner, giving us space to create something new. Since it was not at home, Jack's empty chair did not stare us in the face. Because the feast was a buffet, all of our various dietary needs could be comfortably met, and we did not have to sit around hungrily waiting for our order. Going back and forth to try new dishes gave us something to do, and we recommended choices to one another. We even had a good time conversing cordially, toasting Jack, and chatting with mutual respect for our shared loss.

Having dinner later at a friend's house gave my son, who is an avid and creative cook, a chance to make a couple of dishes to share. This preserved the important piece of cooking favorite foods while relieving us from the chore of preparing a whole meal, setting the table, and cleaning up. We needed this space to take the day a little gently and to acknowledge to one another just how hard it was. Grief is tiring. Not having a lot of extra work made its burden a little easier.

Thoughts

♦ Is there a new or different way to be with loved ones?

♦ Starting to think about a plan early can reduce the stress of celebrations.

♦ It is not necessary to force yourself to feel the expected holiday emotions.

♦ Acknowledge that grief causes fatigue.

The First Year   13

Christmas I

When my first husband died, one of the best pieces of advice I received was, "Do the holidays differently." Clinging to this advice on the first Christmas after Jack died helped me accept that I simply needed to get out of town. I did not want to face putting up the tree and decorating it without him. I especially did not want to take it down alone. Each year, I would want to enjoy the lights for as long as possible, and Jack would be the one to face up to taking the ornaments off and bringing the tree to the curb.

I worried that I would not have the emotional energy to be a loving grandmother on Christmas Day. I felt the weight of somehow trying to be both grandparents in the same way that I remembered trying to be both mother and father when my children's father died. I could not do it then, did not really need to do it then or now, but could not shake the feeling that somehow I should be able to.

There is no way to ignore Christmas. At home, the rituals of Christmas Eve and Christmas Day dinner seemed like chores to be endured, not celebrations of joy, new light, and life the season brings. Yet the rest of us who are alive needed a way to be together on these days of celebration throughout the world. Even though I felt like I would prefer to pass on it, the holiday is real, and it mattered to me and to my family. Being a part of a bereavement group helped. We were asked to make a list of what would be most helpful for the holiday season and to share our lists with one another.

The exercise strengthened my acceptance that finding it all so hard was a part of normal grieving. It gave me support, ideas, and clarity.

A solution came our way because my son-in-law, Dean, had to be in the Texas desert at the MacDonald Observatory over the Christmas week. He was a graduate student astronomer who had to take the time on shared equipment that matched the time the object he was studying was visible at night. Making the plan to join him felt like family building.

Since my daughter, son, and I had never been to West Texas, the trip would not provoke any memories of Jack. An extra benefit was that one of my stepsons, his wife, and twin six-year-old daughters would be able to drive from their home in Austin to spend a few days with us after Christmas. We had a lot of time to put this plan together, so each family member who was involved in the trip could be part of the planning. We rented a small, three-bedroom house with a functional eat-in kitchen and pleasant little living room.

My stepson and his wife spent Christmas as usual in their home, then embarked on the adventure to West Texas. For me, this meant that I did not have to step up as the grandmother I wanted to be until a couple of days after surviving Christmas. For them, it meant a doable plan that included friends and family in Austin and time with us. By the time they arrived, I was eager to see my granddaughters. We had a couple of snuggly sleepovers while the parents had some peace in a hotel.

Travel to Texas simplified gift giving. Jack and I had previously decided that given their ages, gifts no longer made sense for my stepchildren. However, we did continue to give gifts to my children, who always celebrated with us, and to all five grandchildren. Selecting and wrapping gifts for the grandchildren without Jack painfully rubbed in my feeling of loss.

My gift to Dean and Erica was her flight out to Texas and a rental house near the observatory. That way, they could be together on Christmas Eve, Christmas, and cloudy nights when Dean could not work. A plane ticket to an interesting family Texas adventure with accommodations also made a good gift for my son. Everyone agreed that we wanted to have stockings with small gifts to celebrate Christmas morning, that we wanted a live plant symbolic of Christmas in the rented house, and that we wanted to be together. We planned a day that acknowledged both our sadness at Jack's absence and the mystery of the season where dark turns to light.

We followed our usual tradition of celebrating Christmas Eve with a restaurant meal. It helped us through our sense of limited capacity and lack of interest in preparing a special meal. We walked to a restaurant that had a lot of history and enjoyed a fine meal, sharing normal conversation and stories about Jack and how much we missed him. Choosing a place with an interesting history gave us something new to talk about during the meal.

Christmas Day was a gentle day of shared responsibility and love. Dean made an elaborate breakfast for us. We shared the thoughtful and funny gifts we found in our stockings. Dean had been to the area before and knew about hot springs that were about an hour and a half's drive away and were open on Christmas Day. All of us find a great deal of solace and pleasure in nature and are drawn to water, so we agreed that a trip to the hot springs would be a good way to spend the rest of the day.

Travel to the hot springs took us through strange and unfamiliar but beautiful landscapes. The terrain changed dramatically a few times during the drive on progressively smaller and more twisty roads. The last fifteen miles were in a desolate landscape, up a steep dirt and gravel road that threatened to disappear into a passage that our rental car might not manage. Just when I was beginning to feel that we must somehow be in the wrong place, off to the left, down a ravine, we saw lush green trees and a verdant landscape. A little bit farther along, we spotted the hot springs. We had not anticipated experiencing joy in the midst of our painful emotions, but seeing a burst of life in the middle of desolation affected us deeply.

The friendly, easygoing owner greeted us warmly, gave us towels, and showed us around. She was cooking a Christmas dinner for folks from town who would be up later, but she made us most welcome. We sat in an outdoor pool fed by the spring, resting our eyes and spirits by looking out across the ravine at the lovely, peaceful landscape. We spent some time together in the big outdoor hot pool, then the others went off to try the indoor facilities, leaving me much-needed quiet time to contemplate my surroundings and feel what there was to feel inside. When we had all bathed to our satisfaction, we walked over to the dining hall to prepare our picnic. We were very hungry, so the simple foods we had brought seemed like especially delicious treats.

Knowing the roads and where we were going eliminated the terror from the drive back from the hot springs. When we arrived at our little rented home, I made a dinner for all of us. It included things that were special to each person, but it was more like a Sunday supper than a Christmas feast, and it suited us well.

Thoughts

♦ **When a spouse dies, you cannot magically be both of you for children and grandchildren.**

♦ **If it feels too difficult to be home on a big holiday, find a new venue.**

♦ **If doing all of the traditions seems too hard, simplify or do something else instead.**

♦ **Try a bereavement group as a safe place to discuss the upcoming holiday.**

♦ **Determine what the most important part of the holiday is for you.**

♦ **Creating a special ritual of acknowledgment may not be necessary.**

After dinner, we played a board game by the fire and finally were all tired enough to call it a day. We did not do any special ritual, but we were together, had an adventure in which we did something new, shared meals and gifts, and felt free to say what was in our hearts and on our minds.

18

The First Anniversary of Jack's Death

Greg, my niece Brianna, and Devlin were in Rochester with me. Erica and Dean were living in Boston. As the anniversary of Jack's death approached, each of us who had been in the house when he had died experienced a worsening physical sense of anxiety, a feeling that something awful was imminent. We knew the anniversary was coming and knew that it would be a difficult day. But this sense of unmooring was deeper and less conscious than that. Jack's sudden, traumatic death seemed to have left our bodies with a memory based in a sense of the season. Our experiences over the previous year had taught us that milestone days take their toll, whether we choose it or not. Over time, family members became more engaged in the conversation of what to do about each one.

We knew the first anniversary of Jack's death would be tough for all of us. Greg, Erica, and Brianna took part in planning ahead, as each person wanted to be sure that we found a way to collectively honor our feelings of loss. The adults were all clear that it was important to them to have time to talk and grieve without Devlin, as well as time to grieve with him. Grieving with him challenged us to find a way to share and acknowledge the importance of the day without overburdening him or putting him in a situation that was more emotionally challenging than his needs dictated.

The anniversary fell on a Tuesday, which is the day Devlin's singing group rehearses. Carpooling meant that I could drop him off, and he would be returned to us later in the evening. To set the day aside as a significant day for all of us, we planned a dinner together, sharing memories at a small, congenial restaurant we had all enjoyed going to as a family before Jack died. The owner had known and liked Jack. He would understand what we were doing and perhaps even share a memory himself. We also needed the extra benefit of a day off from cooking and cleaning up, as grief was exhausting us.

While thirteen-year-old Devlin attended his vocal group, the adults gathered and made a fire in the fireplace. Erica connected with us via video chat. It was hard for her to be away from us and hard that so few people acknowledged the day. She felt as if friends avoided her for two weeks. She and Dean planned their day carefully. They picked up sandwiches at a favorite Vietnamese sandwich shop and took them to the woods, a place that supported them in honoring Jack. She sent us photos of their woods walk to help us be part of it. The video chat was more successful at making us feel together than we had expected.

Our conversation was light at first, then slowly we centered in and wrote letters to Jack that we burned. Dean greeted us during the chat, but he did not choose to participate in our ritual. His was a background presence for those of us physically gathered and a real presence for Erica. In this instance, just as on Jack's birthday, we found that the writing just happened, the tears flowed easily as we wrote, and a door opened for sharing. There was humor when Erica struggled to find a way to burn her letter. She tried using an ashtray with some herbs in it. At first, it wouldn't light, then a big flame shot up, surprising us all.

Both times that we wrote letters and burned them, we did not realize how the writing would just come out of the pens on its own. Before the event, each of us felt an inner resistance to engaging directly with our grief. It can be so overwhelming, and it is frightening to think we might be pulled back down. The bonding among us as we wrote and the support we felt from the presence of the others were things we knew we needed. Still, making the difficult choice to do it required preplanning and commitment to one another. The experience of doing this together was both deeper than we had expected and an important piece of creating a sense of solidarity in growing into our new lives without Jack.

Thoughts

♦ **Milestones are significant and powerful.**

♦ **Time for adults to grieve separately from children may help.**

♦ **Children may need their own form of support.**

♦ **Others may not acknowledge or realize the power of what the day means for you.**

♦ **Treat resistance to dealing with grief and pain gently.**

♦ **Shared humor is part of a celebration of life.**

When Devlin returned, he readily engaged in the video chat but chose not to write a letter. The dinner honoring his grandfather was enough. He was interested in knowing what we had done, but just being together with us in the present more closely fit his needs. He enjoyed getting a video tour of Erica's carriage house residence and talking about possible plans for the future. Our earlier ritual had lightened the mood enough for us to meet him where he was.

Chapter Two

Sucker Punches and Surprise Challenges

Anticipating Jubilee Week II

The week before Jubilee Week, I found myself unexpectedly shaky. This week, the second time I had faced Mother's Day, my wedding anniversary, and Jack's birthday without him here to celebrate, brought its own challenges. In the preceding months, I had found myself able to be more alive and present in the world. My life at home had grown more functional, often life-giving and at times joyful.

I made what seemed to be a sensible plan to stay at home for these days of the celebration of our marriage and of Jack's presence here on earth. If it was so sensible, why was I so shaky? Why was it so hard to focus or concentrate, and why did it seem so much harder to find the motivation to organize daily tasks?

After much resistance, I turned to writing. Throughout the first year of loss, it seemed to be a way through times when nothing seemed right or when the ground that had seemed to be growing firmer under my feet slipped away. I was forced to recognize that the time leading up to these special days has an agenda that happens with or without my willing participation. At first, I just made a list or outline of a possible plan. The outline made me aware that being home meant I could figure out the plan a day at a time, getting through one occasion before facing the next. But more writing was needed. Next is an excerpt of the writing that helped me make a plan.

First, I know that I become shaky and a little disoriented when there is grief waiting around the corner for me to notice. Grief is making it difficult to ask for help in planning. I cannot say the words "Next Tuesday is my anniversary" without tears. Part of me hates this renewed loss of control. Part of me knows that it is the price of loving.

I know I need to make time for tears. I will be careful this week to mostly be with people who are at ease with deeper conversation and who are not frightened by tears that just arise. I need space and time when I am not task-oriented to let grief emerge. Perhaps this is what all of the disorientation is about. I have to slow down and feel because I am not making a lot of headway focusing on doing or planning. Part of making time is arranging not to have the care of my grandson on my anniversary.

Our anniversary was very important to Jack. Over the years, he brought me to a deeper understanding of why, and its importance grew for me. He would take time off from work to celebrate the actual day. Whether we stayed in town or traveled, we would make plans well in advance for two or three days that would be just ours. Although there were celebratory meals and gifts, Jack was not just a gift-and-out-to-dinner kind of guy. Our anniversary time was a time to step back, celebrate what we had, who we were to each other, and the parts of ourselves that we shared with no other.

Of course, the anniversary included making love and the recognition that this was just for the two of us. We had a strong physical attraction to each other and saw each other as sexy people, as a woman and a man. Physical affection was something that bound our whole selves. All through our marriage, there were always little daily caresses snuck into mundane activities like doing the dishes or cooking; they were a kind of foundation. Our anniversary was a time to set aside our roles of parents, grandparents, and citizens of the world and to explicitly be husband and wife to one another.

It was not always easy to arrange, but each year our plans involved something outdoors, like biking or canoeing or hiking or, when I was very ill, a wheelchair ride through a botanical gardens. We liked adventures, the people we were when we were in natural surroundings, and splurging on a fine meal and lodging. These trips set up a time outside time that was just for us. After Jack's death, I discovered that he had saved every card I had written to him for our anniversary and on his birthday. Of course, I was awash in grief.

The challenge of Jubilee Week was different this year. I found that part of mourning Jack's loss and honoring his life and our lives together was a strong drive to live into whatever it means that I am still alive. Jack and I talked about this at two funerals before we expected either of our deaths to be imminent. But I was finding that the reality takes the same kind of daily attention that our commitment to sustaining and building a loving marriage required.

Thoughts

♦ **Honoring the love you shared includes trying to live fully.**

♦ **Writing may help you know what you are thinking and feeling and what you need.**

It takes time, reflection, imagination, a willingness to take risks, and energy that waxes and wanes day by day. Just as our anniversary was a time to step back and recognize and renew what we had, my sense that something was not right was telling me to try to do the same for my commitment to living life as fully as I can. Yes, it would involve sadness, but maybe there would be joy or humor or a feeling of the fullness of life if I could make room for it.

Jubilee Week II

Last year, the fact that Jubilee Week included Mother's Day slipped by me. This year, it added to the weight. I liked and I missed being a two-parent family and Jack's appreciation for my role as mother and grandmother. The disorientation I felt in the first year after Jack's death was weaker this year but present, and it affected how I could be in the world and what I was able to do.

Last year, Jubilee Week came so close to Jack's death that I was fully aware of my fragility and almost desperate to make a plan to be out of town and with supportive family for the whole week. This year, I did not see an easy way to arrange the week off, and I did not give myself enough space or set up enough loving support. In part, I seem to have bought into the societal acceptance that after a year of grief, it is time to move on. In some inner chamber, I believed it was time that I should be whole. While I knew I wanted to observe the key days of Jubilee Week, I did not know that my sense of being unmoored would return for as long and as power-fully as it did.

The second year brought home the feeling and knowledge that this is forever. He truly will not be back. Surviving the first year does not mean that things will go back to normal. Not only is he gone, but the work to be whole on my own just goes on; missing him just goes on; the need to have him here to comfort me from the pain of losing him just goes on. All of it is sharpened by the days of former celebrations. Paying attention to activities of acknowledgment and healing did help, and it was easier than the first year. But it was still deeply painful.

Mother's Day

On Mother's Day, I had lovely phone conversations with each of my children, received thoughtful gifts, and spent the afternoon and early evening with a friend at a festival in a park listening to good music and walking the paths. Her mother had died a couple of years previously, so our walk included a visit to the memorial bench she'd placed for her mother and grandmother. These things helped pass the day with love and healing.

Wedding Anniversary

Our anniversary was the following Tuesday. Planning a loose framework for the day helped me feel calmer about its approach and helped me acknowledge how important it still was. In the early part of the day, there was self-care. I did my exercises, spent time in the pool, and enjoyed the quiet, beauty, and birds that fill my backyard. A surprise to me was a wish that I acted on to iron the pile of shirts that was sitting on the ironing board and to do a little closet organizing and weeding.

On the Saturday before, I had done a massive purge of my dresser and had taken all of it to Goodwill. My best understanding of these choices was that making external order helped make internal order. Also, it was partly stepping into a new life by making it easier to get dressed in things that fit properly and were in good repair.

Dinner on the anniversary day was with a good friend who had loved Jack and understood our love for each other. This was a planned event to recognize and celebrate my anniversary, but most of our conversation was about the present and future. We shared some laughter, and it had a bit of the feel of a girls' night out.

After our meal, my friend had a rehearsal, and I went to two dance lessons. Needing to wait to see how I felt, I had saved the decision to go until the last minute. Dance lessons are a regular part of what I do to connect with others in a joyful way and to challenge myself with new learning. Also, the physical activity helps my overall sense of wellness. Missing a week of lessons would have made the next week harder, so I wanted to see if I could manage to participate. Before going, I gave myself permission to leave if it was too difficult to focus or to be there. No one at the lessons knew that this was my anniversary. I would not have been able to comfortably handle sympathy.

At one point during the second lesson, I was clearly losing focus, so I stepped out for a few moments. I was not in danger of weeping. It was just a lapse in my ability to concentrate. By the end of the second lesson, I needed to be home and alone to take time to grieve privately. The exercise and connection to others definitely lightened the load and helped to shift my grief from overwhelming to simple mourning.

Jack's Birthday

For me, Jack's birthday meant a chance to do loving things for him. This year, perhaps the loving thing would be caring for his grandson. On the birthday, I held to normal but shortened homeschool responsibilities with my grandson. We had the satisfaction of completing all of the planned work, then went to Mendon Ponds Park. Devlin had gone there many times with Jack, and it was our intention to catch small fish to stock our backyard pond. Devlin used to do this with Jack and felt it would be a good way to honor his grandfather and the day. As part of our preplanning, we had purchased nets the day before, so we set off better prepared than I had been the previous Father's Day.

On the way down to the park, we talked about grief and how it hits you on the special days, whether you expect it or not. We talked about what Devlin was doing that would have made his Poppa happy and proud. There was time for shared sorrow and some tears. Perhaps the length of the drive put an external limit on our discussion that freed us to be frank and to let our feelings come.

At the pond, there were a lot of young children who borrowed my net to help. Devlin kept his net. The help made for added excitement, but the extra action muddied the water too much for successful fish scooping. Devlin felt that this was okay because sharing was the way his Poppa would have done it. We planned to go back the next week and try fishing again. We also had some quiet time in the park, and Devlin commented on how peaceful it was. My unmoored state and need for comfort and a slower pace remained after the end of Jubilee Week, so I was glad we had planned to go back to the park for the fish and for the peace.

The last ritual planned for Jubilee Week, one I did on my own, was to plant the lily bulbs that were special to Jack. He had gotten them from a master gardener's sale at the same festival I had attended on Mother's Day. Each year, he had dug them up and replanted them in the spring. They multiply, so I cannot plant them all. Last year, I gave quite a few away, but I still have more than he started with.

Thoughts

♦ **The passage of time does not eliminate your need for support.**

♦ **Mundane, practical tasks can help.**

♦ **Exercise helps.**

♦ **Think about engaging in an activity that honors a special quality of your loved one.**

Giving them away is a nice way to spread a little of Jack's love. Planting some and watching them grow is a way for me to remember his joy in the garden and my joy in his life.

Sucker Punches: Challenges that Come Out of Nowhere

For over twenty years, every six months, the same dentists and hygienists have cleaned and examined my teeth. For at least ten years, they did the same for both my children. The dentists, a married couple, used my daughter's name when their daughter was born. We seemed to know one another in professional but friendly way.

Three months after Jack died, I went in for a routine cleaning. When I encountered them, the dentist and hygienist each expressed their regret for my loss, but it was quite awkward. At checkout, I gave the receptionist my new insurance information and watched her change the forms. The dentist slowly edged himself behind the glass of the reception area to avoid any conversation about either Jack's death or how I was doing. When I started to say a little about Jack's death to the hygienist, the dentist went inside a small storage room that is behind the glassed-in area. The receptionist sat at her station between us, looking unsure and unhappy as she watched this unfold. It was uncomfortable, but it was only my dentist. They had all offered their condolences. Maybe that was enough.

A year later, my third visit to the office after Jack's death should have been uneventful. The appointment occurred during a time of slowing down. It was a week with few obligations as I transitioned from caring full time for my grandson, Devlin, to feeling my way into new patterns of life on my own. It was a time to reset with extra rest and space to be quiet, a time to notice how my internal life was doing.

While caring for Devlin, I was organized and productive. Since I was acting in the role of parent and homeschool teacher, I needed to be strong enough to be a supportive and focused adult. There was the teaching and general organization involved with feeding a fourteen-year-old regularly and the complicated chauffeuring schedule that caused me to know the inside of my car quite well. Now I was taking a little break from knitting myself together and just kind of checking in to see what life was like without active stitching. I did not expect the visit for routine cleaning to be a challenge.

When I arrived, the receptionist handed me two pieces of paper to update my files. One was basic personal identification and insurance information, and one was a brief health history. I have done those many times. She said that she had filled in the personal form as much as possible from my records and that I probably just needed to check them. I sat down in the nicely appointed waiting area, with its soothing but attractive art, and began checking the form.

When I got to the section for responsible party, there was my husband's name, L. Jackson Fraser. All the information about him was filled in with details that were true sixteen months ago. I started to shake, tears streamed down my face, and I was finding it hard to breathe. He is not here to be responsible or to answer the call if a medical emergency arises. He is not here to share a hug and give his report of his day or ask for mine. What was his name doing on this form? I crossed out all of the places where the form held its lies and wrote in "self."

Self is the correct answer except for the times when a sucker punch comes out of nowhere. Luckily, there was no one else in the reception area. Since it was the dentist's office, and since I already knew that they did not do grief or loss well, I tried just focusing on my breath until I slowly came back into control. This was a well-practiced skill a year ago, but not one I'd needed recently. I caught a glimpse of the dentist and receptionist through the glass, and it looked like they were just leaving me alone until things were smoother. Unable to discuss it and not wanting to get the receptionist in trouble, I used the glue of breath to recreate an external house to protect the soft inhabitant within. When I eventually completed the forms and passed them back to her, she thanked me with commonplace, medical office–distracted courtesy.

Thoughts

♦ **Many people will not know how to acknowledge your grief.**

♦ **Grief bursts will happen, but they don't last long.**

♦ **Remember to breathe.**

When I was in the dental chair, the hygienist looked over the form and noticed what I had crossed out. He tsk-tsked softly at the receptionist's error but said nothing. All of our conversation was gentle, light, and easy. The dentist came in to examine my teeth and was friendly and outgoing. The receptionist checked me out and made my next appointment with courtesy and a pleasant demeanor.

Not a word was spoken about what everyone knew had occurred.

Father's Day II

A couple of weeks before the second Father's Day after Jack's death, the by-now familiar feeling of disorientation, compromised focus, and sense of confusion returned as it had prior to each of the milestone days. It is as if my body feels there is something not right about what is coming. The feeling is less unmooring as time goes by but very real. I was more functional, and knowing I'd worked through this last year reminded me to let the feelings guide me. They are a reminder that this is a time for gentleness and simpler expectations, a time for feeling, and maybe a time to look at photos or listen to music that releases grief's tears.

A psychologist who spoke to my bereavement group said that the sense of disorientation is because there is sadness that needs to be felt. I agree, but I think it is more than that. I think it is partly a sense that there is something I should be doing or planning or something I am forgetting to do. For so many years, my focus was on trying to figure out just the right thing to do to make the day special. The kids would have consulted about what they could do from a distance, and we would have shared the fun of a clandestine conspiracy. The holiday heightens the sense of missing Jack but also the loss of being able to do something appreciative and loving.

My son and daughter also found that they were facing some disorientation and renewed grief. Greg phoned around this time, finding that the ads that showed up in his email showing him things he could do for his father were triggering his grief. Erica made arrangements to be here in Rochester, in part because she felt the need for us to be together on this day. We found ourselves reaching out to reconnect. Maybe we were steadying each other; maybe we were strengthening our sense of connection; perhaps we were just needing to touch the ones we loved who also loved Jack.

My son lived in St. Louis, far from Rochester, so we looked for ways to share the day. He started the connection when he sent us a photo of carrot pancakes he had made in honor of Jack, who loved carrot cake. We sent back photos of the shards of a vase that had sentimental value to Jack and to me that we were gluing back together. One anniversary, Jack and I had purchased the vase and its wrought-iron holder from a small shop owned by a man we had come to like. Our affection for the pot grew when the shop owner closed the establishment to move to Mexico and marry the woman who'd sold him the pot.

Another large pot from this store had housed a tropical plant in Jack's office. Unfortunately, the pot broke and the plant died when we'd brought it home. For Father's Day, we organized ourselves to repair these broken things and create wholeness where there was brokenness.

Until it had broken, the smaller pot had held one of only two houseplants we own. Jack had brought the plant to the marriage, and I strove to keep it alive. I had never been successful at sustaining houseplants but was learning and took some pride in my success so far. During the winter, the plant lived in the house. It went out to summer camp when the weather warmed up. A friend had accidentally knocked it down, breaking the pot in the same place it had broken the last time it fell.

Erica and I felt it would not be strong enough to hang in its decorative iron holder anymore, so we designed a complicated project for the day. We planned to find a new pot for the holder, a plant for the new pot, a plant and new base for the repaired pot, and a fitting pot for the treasured remaining houseplant. We also planned to repair the base of the large pot from Jack's office, so we could fill it with lilies that had come as a gift when he died. Our project gave us lots of time together, doing tasks that did not involve too much thinking. They did involve beauty, creativity, and transformation of disorder into new combinations of whole inanimate and living things. It honored a part of Jack that we loved and the parts of us that loved loving him.

Since glue takes time to dry, and shopping takes more time than I ever expect, we only partially completed our project. We were satisfied with the progress we'd made and the safe transfer of Jack's plant to a new and beautiful pot. We had all of the other components in place and were able to finish the project over the course of the following week.

Our Father's Day also included a walk in Highland Park to check out the memorial benches that people have placed

Thoughts

- **Disorientation and confusion are indications to slow down, be gentle with yourself, and simplify or reduce expectations.**

- **Reconnect with those who share your loss.**

- **Try being in a natural setting or planting something.**

- **Maybe you can bring order out of chaos in one small way.**

there for loved ones who have died. I wanted to show Greg and Erica the bench my friend had placed for her mother and grandmother and some of the other memorial benches that are placed throughout the park. Each bench has a small plaque with an inscription about the person it honors. Erica and I sent photos of a couple of benches to Greg so that the three of us could converse about the benches before I chose wording for the inscription on a bench for Jack and called the parks department to order it.

Erica and I ended our day with a swim in the lake. We both love to swim and find great peace being in the water and near a lake. Also rhythmic and smooth exercise helps us sleep. My son ended his day drumming in a drum circle he had participated in many times before. We honored our loss and honored our continuing lives.

Chapter Three

Planning, Preparing for, and Performing the Ash-Scattering Ceremony

Spring and Summer 2012

Long before Jack died, he wrote a letter requesting that as many family members as were able gather in Canada's Algonquin Park to scatter his ashes. Our family committed to finding a way to honor his wish, but the logistics were a real challenge. We needed to make a plan that accommodated differing freedom to travel, varying comfort levels with camping, and a wide range of needs for connection to the wilderness.

Finding ways to accommodate everyone meant creating two
different but connected strategies.

Ten of us planned to meet seventeen months after Jack's
death for a weekend at a campground in the park. We would
gather on Friday night, do our ash-scattering ritual on Saturday, then go our separate ways on Sunday. We were able to
preplan the dates and location for the trip but could not work
out specific details until we all met in the Algonquin.

Four of the ten—Erica, Dean, my granddaughter Alana,
and I—felt the need to prepare our souls and spend time in
the wilderness portion of Algonquin Park. We decided to go
to the park on the Monday preceding the larger family event
for a five-day, four-night canoe trip into the interior wilderness of the park. Then we would join the others in the campground. The following sections are a description of the process
of planning these two trips and the ceremony, the story of our
small group wilderness trip, and a description of our experience during and after the ceremony. The ceremony itself can
be found in the appendix at the end of the book.

Planning the Written Ceremony and the Logistics of the Gathering

Following through on Jack's wish to have our family gather
in Algonquin Park to scatter his ashes felt like the last act of
kindness that I could offer him. Perhaps the daily exchange
of small kindnesses is what I miss most since his death, and
getting this one right mattered all the way down to my core.

I wanted to help us gather in a way that respected all of us with our challenges of distance, health, and finances. I wanted to create a process that made space for us to be together in our grief and our loss, had room for individual expression and quiet, and, most of all, helped us each to say good-bye. If things worked out as I hoped, we would find some peace, some comfort from one another, a little movement toward appreciating the joy of Jack's life, and release of some of our sorrow.

There were a surprising number of tasks to be accomplished. To preserve my energy and limit the times I had to confront the grief that planning awoke, I tried to do the structural tasks using a group email process. For most of the family, this was not really satisfactory. They preferred the more personal connection of phone conversations, so we ended up with a balance of the two. I think that everyone struggled with the wish to postpone thinking about what we were planning to do. Once postponed, answering emails drops off the radar. More than that, though, email can feel impersonal, and we were planning an event that was about connection to one another and to our loss.

To make this work, we needed to agree on dates, number of campsites, and a location in the park. Finding a time that worked for as many family members as possible meant that our ceremony took place seventeen months after Jack's death. After gathering information about times that would work the best, I took responsibility to set a firm date and make the reservation at a campground in the park. The reservation needed to be made the first day it was possible, so everyone needed to let me know how many of their nuclear family members were coming and how many tents they would bring a week or so before a five-month deadline. Then I needed to call the park and do the best I could to find us campsites near one another in a campground that would be a good base for us. Payment for all sites had to be made with the reservation.

Family members came from Texas, Missouri, Massachusetts, and New York. Small groups made arrangements to share camping supplies, do a little meal planning, meet at the airport, and acquire canoes. They found the group email was valuable for this sort of planning. It also helped in getting input for the service.

To plan the service, I requested information from others about what they would like to see happen. I felt it was my responsibility to create our ceremony. Part of that responsibility was to ensure that it was inclusive and met the needs of all of us. Our group ranges from active practicing Catholics, to believers who find occasional comfort in the rituals of religion, to folks who know that they believe in something but feel that the scope of the meaning of a spiritual life may be too big to be understood.

My daughter, who is a musician, offered us a song and shared a recording of it so that everyone could be familiar with the melody before singing along at the ceremony. My oldest stepson, Aaron, reflected on his father's wish to have his formal memorial service follow the Episcopal Book of Common Prayer and did some Internet research on possible prayers to open and close the ash-scattering ceremony. My younger stepson, David, searched unsuccessfully for a letter his father had sent him, but in the end he felt that he would be able to come up with something else to share. I searched the Internet, my heart and memory, and my experience of the flow of things in rituals to put together the ceremony.

It took me days of gathering and sifting through written material and sitting in silence to let music come into my voice. I needed one day of being alone to focus on putting the ceremony together; then I needed to show it to Brianna, Alana, and a good friend to know that it met my goals. Since we would be outside, Alana helped me put a copy for each person in a plastic three-ring binder. I found and copied a recent photo of Jack on an island in the Algonquin, which we glued to the inside front cover of each person's binder.

Another puzzle was how to accomplish the physical task of scattering the ashes in a way that would best put people at ease. A friend cautioned me that scattering in the wind can cause the ashes to blow back into your face. Another friend shared his experience that some family members would need to take a little time alone, while others might want to scatter the ashes together. He also explained that I would need a container with a relatively wide neck. Some folks suggested using a large spoon, and some cautioned care with potential squeamishness about bone fragments. Some mentioned using gloves as a way to pick up handfuls of ashes. Others found the idea of handling the ashes directly too uncomfortable.

It was good to get all of this information. It let me see how wide the range of natural reactions to this process would be, and it helped me plan a way to make it comfortable for individuals to choose their own method. I purchased two inexpensive blue florist's wide-mouth vases that could be used for pouring or for removing the ashes by hand.

Thoughts

♦ **Limit the number of logistical details you must plan ahead.**

♦ **Creating a respectful ceremony is an act of deep love, but it brings up deep pain.**

♦ **It is natural to procrastinate about such a meaningful and challenging task.**

♦ **Take the time to think about what you want help with and what you need to do on your own.**

The Wilderness Trip

At every step of the way, each of us struggled with the avoidance, procrastination, and confusion that accompanied us for each major event following Jack's death.

This time, though, planning was essential. For the small group wilderness trip, our physical well-being was dependent on accomplishing tasks such as planning the route, reserving our camping sites on the lakes in the interior of the park, figuring out what gear and clothing to bring, and planning and purchasing enough food to sustain us as we paddled and hiked our way from lake to lake.

In the end, our route was close to perfect; we brought too much food, approximately the right amount of gear, and just enough clothing. We also brought attitudes of love for one another, the wilderness we were visiting, and the process of exploring the lakes and trails as we tested our muscles and skills. We arrived with just enough time to canoe and portage one lake in and set up our camp before darkness fell. From the moment I stepped into the first lake, I felt as if I had come home.

Alana and Erica had both attended the same girl's canoe-ing camp in the park. An important part of their camp was singing for everything from mealtime to paddling. As we set out on our first morning in the park, Alana, who was the stern paddler in my canoe, asked if it would be okay if she sang as we paddled. Her strong, beautiful voice moved us along with songs that came from her heart. Erica knew some of the same camp songs, Alana taught us others, and Jack's presence was everywhere. The lyrics of one song told how when camp time was done, the singer would send her children and grandchildren to the park, and the traditions would continue.

As we paddled, I saw how wise Jack had been to send us all into the Algonquin, with its strong rocks, lakes that could be peaceful and tranquil or shrouded in rain or fog, wind and waves to fight, thick forests, and terrain that changed from lake to lake and river bend to river bend. We stopped early on the second day at a site that was good for swimming and fishing and took our time leaving the next day. We were drawn into the slower rhythm of camping life and the joys of being on the water.

On our third night, we found a campsite that had a large granite rock sloping gently down to the lake. On the rock, someone had built an Inuit stone sculpture much like the one in my front yard. The rock called to me; its power drew me to sit in a meditation that came as peacefully and easily as taking a stroll. The quiet strength of the stone, the gentle lapping of the waves, the smell of the air, and the feel of the breeze took me in and brought me to a place of wholeness I had not dwelt in for a long time.

On our fourth day, the rain came down on and off all day, sometimes just as a mist, sometimes full on, hard, and steady. Toward the end of the day, when we were all thoroughly cold and wet and tired, it just poured. Trying to get to a place to camp before the rain could make its way through the trees and soak the ground, we aimed for campsite after campsite, only to see a canoe in the distance pull in and take the spot.

At last, we came to a spot that was up a very steep hill and did not look desirable. But we decided to take it no matter what. I hiked up the hill to the tent areas, then hiked a little higher up. There, in the middle of the woods, in the middle of nowhere, was a perfectly constructed tall chimney with a wide hearth and a dry interior filled with dry kindling. The hearth became home for a roaring fire that cooked our food and gave us a place to gather and dry one side at a time.

This day, I was exhausted and retired to the warmth of my sleeping bag as soon as possible after we'd set up and eaten. I had finished reading my book the day before but was content to just lie in the dark, warm and dry. Then came the unexpected part. The sense of being at home, the experience of the power of the quiet beauty, and the separation from all things electronic had been working their way into me. I was becoming more alive, more connected to the earth. As I lay there, my skin felt alive. My last two trips to the Algonquin had been romantic adventures with Jack, and my body remembered.

The next morning, we broke camp, sang and paddled and portaged our way to the canoe rental dock. We shared some of our extra food with other travelers as we joked about carrying it through the whole trip. The wilderness had strengthened me for the next step, leading the ritual of scattering Jack's ashes. It had brought both peace and a new sense of vitality. Still, I was reluctant to leave the peace and rhythm of canoe tripping for the more complex and demanding task that lay ahead.

Reluctant or not, it was time. On Friday, we emerged from our wilderness journey, piled our wet gear into the van, and went to the campground where we were to meet the rest of the group. At my campsite, we emptied the van and placed our wet gear at the bottom of the trunk. In the process, I extracted the cardboard box containing the plastic box of ashes from the funeral home, the vases, and the binders for the ceremony. The box had been well hidden beneath all of the camping gear. As I brought it to the front of the car, I found myself doubled over in grief, shaking, crying, and gasping for air. What we were doing had become real. My daughter came upon me in this state and held me until it passed.

Thoughts

- **Grief bursts can surprise you.**
- **Think about what feeds your soul.**
- **Do you need to be in a supportive environment for the days leading up to a ceremony of remembrance or good-bye?**
- **Notice the times when parts of you are coming back to life.**

It was raining at the campground, and I had no strength to be with the others or set up my tent. I slept in the van on the warm, comfortable backseat with the box of Jack's ashes at my side. I don't know quite what this was about. It felt like the vigil we might have held with Jack's body had it not been whisked away for autopsy. Maybe it was just a last night together. Whatever the explanation, I needed to protect and be with the ashes as part of a sacred duty.

Planning the Location and Timing of Our Ceremony

Our group was able to preplan only the overall logistics of the trip to Algonquin Park. We waited until we were all there to agree on how much paddling people wanted to do and what time to set off from the campground. Alana, Erica, and I had preplanned two possible routes for finding a place to scatter Jack's ashes; one was relatively easy and involved putting the canoes in right where we were, and one involved two short portages and canoeing across three lakes. We posed these options to the family. The consensus was that we had come there to make a trek into the park, so we would drive the canoes to the first lake and do the more strenuous route.

The weather report was for rain, sometimes hard and sometimes just a mist, and the threat of an occasional thunderstorm. We agreed that we could not let the rain determine our plan, so after lunch we set off for the first lake.

The group included my three stepchildren, my two children, my son-in-law, my niece, my sixteen-year-old granddaughter and fourteen-year-old grandson, and me. We set out in four canoes and paddled in light rain across the first lake, the channel to the next lake, and the second lake. With everyone helping everyone, we carried our gear across the first portage in a pouring rain only to observe thunder and lightning over the lake at the end of our portage.

We stood chatting, sheltered by the trees and canoes, and watched the storm, hoping it would let up enough for us to continue. We toyed with the idea of leaning the canoes together to make enough shelter to conduct our ritual there, but no one wanted to stop the quest until we had reached our goal. So, when the thunder and lightning disappeared, we canoed across a small lake to a short portage to Little Island Lake, where we hoped to have our ceremony. Leadership on these paddles and portages was shared, and decisions seemed to happen of their own accord.

When we got to Little Island Lake, David led the way to a campsite that was perfect. It had a large open area around a fire ring, as well as an area that was sheltered by trees in case the rain persisted. Shortly after we arrived on the site, the rain cleared, the sun came out, and the sky became a mix of clear, blue patches and puffy, white cumulous clouds.

Thoughts

♦ **If possible, let go of planning every detail in advance.**

♦ **Give someone the job of ensuring that there will be food to share.**

The first thing we did was eat. Greg and Brianna brought out bean salads, tofu, chips, and other energizing food they had packed from home for all of us to share. Aaron had brought grapes that were reminiscent of an important part of his and his siblings' childhood camp experiences with their dad. We needed to eat after all of our exertion, but also nurturing one another, sharing food, and struggling together to get to this spot were part of creating the ceremonial space we needed.

Aaron and I stepped off into the woods and filled the vases; then we began.

Letting Go of Jack's Ashes

I opened the ceremony, then asked Aaron to read the first prayer. It was a prayer selected from those he had found on the Internet. Brianna read a Ralph Waldo Emerson piece she had selected. Erica, Devlin, and I led the first song. We sang the chorus a couple of times first to give everyone a chance to sing along. Music at this point helped us slow down, come together as a group, and move to a space more in our hearts and less in our heads.

Next, in the time for sharing, David read something he had written. He first spoke about how much he would have liked to call his dad for advice over the last year as he purchased a home and worked to make repairs. Then he shared that his favorite part of church when he was a child was when prayers would be offered from the pulpit, and the congregation would respond, "Lord hear our prayer." He said he liked it, because he knew what to do.

He then extracted a small notebook from under his poncho and shared a number of humorous and touching qualities of the person his dad had been. He asked us to respond, "Lord hear our prayer" to each of the items he read. The list included "for those who view a half a bushel of beets as an asset" and ended with "for Lawrence Jackson Fraser." Greg spoke about how, while he was mourning the loss of all Jack might have taught him in the future, on this trip he had grown to more deeply understand how Jack continued to be a presence in his life.

I read a message to the grandchildren with an explanation about how they might not have known how much their grandfather had loved them, talked about them, been proud of them, and been always interested in who they were and what they were doing. One of the things he had done with each grandchild was read stories, so I selected a piece from a book they might have read.

Then it was time for scattering the ashes. First, I spoke a bit about what I had learned from friends about the process. I focused on how each person might have different needs and that people could take turns going to a private place to leave some ashes or that we could do it in small groups or together or that anyone could choose to take some back with them if they wished. I taught everyone a chant and explained it as something to carry us through the time while people took their time scattering ashes. I only had two containers, and there were lots of us, so the process was slow.

At first, I was leading the chant, but as I tired, different voices took up the lead, and no one let it die. In the beginning, it was clear to me that we were singing it for Jack. Then it began to feel as if we were singing it for one another. The slow process of going off into the woods as individuals gave us lots of space to group and regroup, offering a hand to hold or our arms around one another for support. After we had all taken a turn, we reconvened, and Elizabeth read the final prayer. We ended joined in a circle hug that turned into a bit of the hokey pokey.

Even after we had each taken a turn, we still had lots of ashes left. The tension of the day had gone. We had done what we had to do and were now more free to do what came naturally. My daughter gathered a group and scattered some of the ashes in the fire ring of the campsite. She wanted to add the elements of fire and air even though it would not happen until someone camped there. My grandson took some ashes in his hand and brought them down to the water to let them float away.

We took the rest of the ashes out in the canoes and formed a sort of square by holding onto one another's canoes. Those who wished to take some out by hand did so, and others just lowered the vases into the water to let the ashes float away. They were strangely beautiful in the clear darkness of the water.

As we finished and began canoeing toward home, the rains returned. Again we had to fight the elements. Paddling songs were sung, toothless threats of splashing were made from boat to boat by people who could not have been any wetter, and we made our way back to our cars. While most folks went to drop off canoes, Greg and Brianna built a large fire back at the campground and started a meal that could be shared by all.

We just sat around eating and telling stories. Some were about Jack, some were just stories. Herring was served in Jack's honor. Jiffy Pop, which has a warning on the label that says that it cannot be popped over an open flame, was popped to perfection over the fire because Jack would have done that. Marshmallows were burned in honor of all of the burned marshmallows Jack's kids had passed to him over the years. Grandchildren fed the flames of the fire, and, eventually, one by one, people retired.

Thoughts

♦ **Let the structure bring you into sacred space.**

♦ **If you are scattering ashes, acknowledge that people may have different needs and comfort with the process.**

♦ **Make room for all to participate if they wish.**

We all went our own way the next day, but there was peace among us; we felt that we had truly done something hard and meaningful. Family thanked me for our ritual. For me, completing this last obligation seemed to let things I had been holding in drain out of my body. There was exhaustion but relaxation, a sharper sense of grief but a stronger sense of entering into new life, a heightened awareness of Jack's presence but a sense that his presence was becoming more diffuse. Perhaps, in scattering his ashes as a family, we had begun to let him go.

Chapter Four

The
Holidays
Revisited

Thanksgiving II

The second Thanksgiving after Jack died came with a set of needs that were different from the challenges of previous holidays. For the first time, I had no responsibility to be part of or plan a family celebration. My adult children were observing the holiday with their significant others, my niece who lived with me was heading off to be with her family, and it felt like a chance to breathe.

The usual preholiday anxiety and disorientation came to visit, but I felt drawn to the idea of four days of seeing what it would be like to just follow my nose. In the past, having a plan and a reason to focus in advance tempered my anxieties and decreased holiday stress. This time, the freedom not to plan or to step up for others reduced my preholiday anxious anticipation.

On Thanksgiving eve, a friend I got to know after Jack died stopped by to pick up something. He ended up staying for a simple supper and some deep conversation. The topic was his; I was primarily a listener. The quiet space inside the empty house made room for this unexpected shared experience that deepened our friendship and lessened my sense of being alone in the world.

My extended family held a big Thanksgiving dinner four hours from my home. I was invited and could have ridden there with my niece. The family is a lively group. I knew the meal would be full of animated conversation and abundant good food. After dinner, there would be games and laughter. Yet I did not want to go. The thought of it just made me tired. I did not feel up to stepping into the role I have in that family, even though it is a good role with people I love. I did not want to join in the very active socializing or to be away from my home and interacting with others for a whole weekend.

I felt a bit like I had when I'd first come home from college, knowing I had changed and not knowing how to fit. My new self hadn't been strong enough then, and the self I was developing as a newly single person needed more breathing space to emerge. I could not picture myself at the event. I was both surprised and delighted by the idea that I could choose to go or not to go. It had never occurred to me before.

Not following the automatic choice of traveling to be with family left room for new things to happen. Once friends knew I would be on my own, I had multiple invitations to dinner. Thanksgiving seems to be a holiday with meals big enough to share and a sense of hospitality that extends to those who are on their own. I felt loved and strengthened in my hope that I could build a new life by each of these invitations. One was to a family dinner; one to a meal with a group of adults who spend many holidays together; and one from a male friend to join him at a dinner of mixed family and friends.

My friendship with this man was not romantic, but I liked the idea of going as his companion for the meal. It felt important to figure out a new way to attend events with a man who was not my husband or my lover. Also, I was drawn to the idea of meeting new congenial people in a low-key setting. There, I could be just a person, a new friend, not a widow who was grieving her way through yet another special day filled with reminders of loss. I could be quiet and listen or engage when it felt right.

Thanksgiving Day I woke late and spent some restorative time in the woods. While I was walking, I realized that part of grace at the meal might be to say what we were thankful for. So I turned my attention to gratitude. Immediately, my sense of gratitude for the life I'd had with Jack came flooding in with vivid memories of tender times, tough times, joys, shared struggles, struggles we did not know how to share, the twinkle in his eye when he played with a child, and times he was a real dad to my children. Of course, along with gratitude, these memories brought sorrow and tears.

The woods and the pace of the day gave me space for a quiet time to let all of it happen without the need to be anything for anyone. As my emotions played themselves out, my attention slowly turned to the present and to what I might be willing to share in my disguise as a person who just happened to be free for the holiday.

There were obvious things, such as the health I am regaining, the gentle people who invited me to share the day with them, the ability to stay in my home, family, the woods, the sky, and the sound of the creek. To my surprise, what emerged most strongly was a deep appreciation for parks, and the way they give us all free and easy access to the wilderness and ourselves. This would be easy to share comfortably, so I was prepared for going to dinner. Thinking about gratitude would turn out to be part of every day of my Thanksgiving weekend.

When I got back from the woods, I chatted on the phone with each of my stepsons and made two simple dishes to bring to the dinner. I did not worry about providing enough vegetarian food for the vegetarians in my extended family or about being sure that there were choices for everyone's dietary restrictions. I just made dishes I liked.

My hosts were pleasant and welcoming; it was easy to just sit back and listen or engage in conversation. The home was lovely, and learning about its history of fire and renovation provided an easy way to become part of the group. Helping a little in the preparation and cleanup also added to my comfort.

After dinner, I had a walk and a chat with one of the other single women there. Since I was far out in the country, away from the light pollution of the city, I stopped the car on the way home to lie out on the hood and gaze at the night sky with its millions of stars. I felt proud of the accomplishment of having had a good day, relieved that weeping was not the dominant activity for the day, and deeply grateful for the way my inner work and the support of others gave me a window into an adult life that could have its own satisfactions.

Friday, I again spent some time in the woods, since it always heals me; discovering that I enjoy walking *alone* in nature is new. Friday evening, a little of Saturday afternoon, and Saturday evening, I attended the annual Rochester contra dance festival. Dancing there had helped a lot the previous year, so this was a simple decision to make. I attended when I wanted to and as much as I wanted to, chatted or danced as much as I felt like in the moment, and left when I needed to.

I am acquainted with a lot of the dancers who regularly attend the festival, the tunes and dances are familiar, and the room is always full of smiling, welcoming people, so I feel a sense of coming home and comfort just walking in the door. The music is full of life; it made me move, and it made me grin. The dancers share a joy of dance with one another, and there is little need to talk, because the communication is in the dancing.

At the festival, I am a dancer more than a widow. Most of the people I encountered probably did not even know. There were chances to catch up a bit with old friends and chat with folks I'd only just met. Being in the atmosphere created by hundreds of smiling people and moving to good music brought me joy and accelerated the way my heart was opening to the spirit of Thanksgiving. A dancing bonus is becoming tired enough to sleep easily.

Thoughts

♦ **Be open to honoring your own needs.**

♦ **Trust yourself to figure it out.**

♦ **Do a bit of what restores you.**

♦ **You may need space to cry.**

♦ **Is there an activity that might bring you joy?**

♦ **You may find a shift in the balance of turning to the present and looking back at what you've lost.**

Christmas II

A feeling of defiance toward grief and an anger at its ability to shanghai my life rose up as the second Christmas after Jack died approached. Greg, Erica, Dean, and I decided we wanted to be able to be at my home over the holidays. Our decision came from a mix of not feeling the energy to travel, not wanting to spend money on travel, and the strong sense of wanting to fully inhabit my home and live into our current reality.

The home is a place full of memories of past Christmases, and we were not strong enough to face that the first year. This year, we hoped, would be the year we could embrace it as our family home and the place that could ground us as we moved into our changed family. The idea was frightening, and we gave a lot of thought to creating something new.

We found strength and comfort from thinking and planning together. We were becoming practiced at balancing our mixed needs. We wished to honor the importance Jack held in our lives, make room to celebrate the day, honor our lives as they are, and make space for the full richness of being alive.

To set a tone and make my home welcoming, a week or so before family came home, I strung lights in the trees outside. Jack had done this in years past. Doing it myself was both difficult to face and very satisfying to accomplish. I sent photos of the lights twinkling in the snow to all who would be coming.

I waited for Greg to arrive before getting the tree. It felt too hard to do alone, and he loves doing it. When we moved to the city, Jack and I began a tradition of walking over to the Boy Scout's tree sale and walking the tree home. Greg flew into town the day before the nearby sale shut down so that we could carry on the tradition. His girlfriend joined us in our tree quest. Her presence added new life to the tradition. Plus, she took her turn carrying one end of the tree.

The next challenge was decorating the tree. We waited until Dean and Erica came into town, because it was important to them to participate and so that we could support one another in this ritual that Jack had usually led. We found it difficult to begin and sort of edged ourselves into the activity. We made a fire, then took our time. I sat back and watched as Greg and Erica worked on the lights for the tree, while Dean strung more outside.

There was laughter as Greg and Erica figured out how to string the lights. As we placed ornaments and talked about some of them and their history, we began to have fun and enjoy the beauty we were creating. Earlier, I had purchased an ornament in Jack's honor, and Greg had bought a humming-bird ornament for me. He felt strongly about the rightness of the beauty of the bird, its ability to seek out sweetness, and the nature of its flight.

To lighten our anxiety about holiday meals with the glar-ingly empty chair, we elected to change the meal traditions. I feared the weight of tradition would drive me down too hard. For Christmas Eve, instead of our usual restaurant meal, we decided to cook together. Greg planned a complicated menu that included lots of tasks for everyone, so we could work together on an activity that carried us through the evening.

Elizabeth and Devlin came over in the late afternoon and joined in making the meal, hanging out, and getting the table ready. At dinner, we chose chairs that were not our custom-ary chairs. I asked us to make a toast to Jack, as the person who had brought us all together. I asked that everyone say the name they had for him as we raised our glasses. This turned out to be hard, especially for my fourteen-year-old grandson, but he was grateful that we did it. Once we had acknowledged

Jack with our toast, it was easier to move on to other topics and enjoy the meal.

Having a meal we had not eaten before and that had many new dishes gave us conversation starters. After the meal, we shared small gifts. There was a lot of delight and laughter in sharing gifts that were thoughtful but not pricey.

A friend brought me to a late-night church service that included carols to sing. It ended after midnight, so the first "Merry Christmases" for me were with a group of unrelated folks. The service left me feeling gently transformed. Walking out to giant snowflakes drifting down over every surface brought me deeper into the wonder of the season.

The thought of Christmas Day came with such a strong sense of having the floor disappear that I entertained a wish to spend the day with my head buried under the covers. Planning an alternate way to celebrate the day did not completely dispel this wish, but it did give me hope and grounding enough to choose to be part of the day instead of just surviving it. We planned to have an open house in the evening and each invite friends and their families. We discovered that lots of people are kind of at a loss for what to do on Christmas evening, and people who were in town were delighted to be invited. We found a new shape for the day, and it changed everything.

In the late morning, Greg, Erica, Dean, and I exchanged gifts. At one point, I asked everyone to think about a gift, tangible or intangible, that Jack had given them. I spoke about how he had loved me through all stages of illness and wellness,

Thoughts

♦ **Do something concrete to honor your loved one's role in your life.**

♦ **Can you create something that fits your current reality?**

♦ **There is a balance you can find that honors your loss and your life.**

♦ **Seek out the sweetness in the day.**

♦ **Let go of any tradition that brings more pain than pleasure.**

♦ **Acts of honoring your loved one are difficult to do but gratifying once you've done them.**

♦ **What might give you hope that some part of the day could be celebratory?**

never forgetting who I was. This was a challenging way to begin, but it was a start, and others slowly joined in. The conversation let each of us know more about one another and about Jack. It brought his loving presence into the room. Knowing we had to get the house ready for our open house kept this part of the day from feeling as if it would go on forever and gave us a good reason to get up and change our focus.

Guests came and went throughout the evening. Their pleasure in participating in our event gave us a sense that we were doing something good and convinced us to make it our new tradition. People of different ages and from a number of different countries and families came and got to know one another. Spontaneous games, dancing, and shifting groups of conversation filled our home with lightness, humor, warmth, and joy.

Chapter Five

The Second
Anniversary
of Jack's Death

Anticipating the Anniversary

The second anniversary of Jack's death loomed on the horizon for months in advance. A trip to Texas to visit grandchildren had to be preplanned so that I could be back home for a while before the anniversary day. My children, my niece Brianna, and I all were nervous about what the day would bring. I was angry about having the calendar dictate my capability, yet I knew that it would. I could only hope it would not knock me down too hard or for too long.

So much of me was getting on with living life, and the acute reality of death only strengthened my strong desire to live the life I have. My wish to try new things, expand my boundaries, feel exuberance and inner freedom, engage more deeply, and live more fully was and is exploding out of me. I knew that part of this, the part I did not want to face, the part that was coming whether I chose it or not, was the upcoming anniversary date of Jack's death. Some inner calendar was keeping track, and a sense that something wrong was about to happen slowly grew.

Even if I managed to feel whole on this day, or even if I wished to ignore it, there were other family members to consider. As we approach each of these significant days, I am struck by how my grief is different yet the same as theirs. They wish to support me, and I wish to support them. We are learning how to do this and loving one another more deeply as we do. But I am sick of this being the task that is before us. I wish our planning efforts were going into parties for upcoming graduations or trips, or that we were able to comfortably be more spontaneous and easy. Perhaps I am just angry at death.

The Anniversary

We talked about the upcoming anniversary, and all agreed that we would carve out space to be gentle to ourselves and to one another and to find a way to be together. On his way home from work on the day he died, Jack had gathered sticks to be used for kindling in our wood stove. We had preserved this stash of sticks for two years now and decided that on March 7 we would use them to make a fire. It was time. My daughter and niece were here with me, and my son was in St. Louis, so we agreed on a time that we could video chat with him.

To honor my own need to keep doing the things that are bringing me joy and satisfaction, I went to my salsa lessons at six and seven that evening. Maybe I just needed to pretend for a while that life was fine, or maybe I needed to live a part of my life that is fine. I let the instructor know ahead of time that I might not be able to manage the classes but wanted to try.

It ended up being pleasant and a way to let go of physical tension and feel normal for little while. I know the others in the group as good acquaintances as we have struggled to learn the salsa moves together. I was surprised that I was able to sit and chat after the lessons and mention why the day was a hard one for me. I did not lose it, although I think that a few tears would have been fine. Mostly, there was compassion. One student had recently lost a friend and needed to talk about that and about the death of another friend some time ago. Even though it was maybe not the best time for me to be a good listener, it mattered to listen.

When I got home, we made hot chocolate and popcorn, initiated the video chat, then started the fire. We wanted our snack to be one of Jack's favorite foods, but since they were herring, anchovies, sardines, and the like, we settled on popcorn as one of the few that we found palatable. For a couple of hours, we shared stories. They were mostly happy or funny stories and included many that only one or two of us knew.

Each of us knew a different Jack. Brianna had worked for him at the university for four years, Erica and Greg had had many different adventures with him, and, of course, I knew lots of things that they did not know. There were also the stories that we just wanted to recount that all or most of us knew. This seemed like a perfect acknowledgment of the day. Our time together wound down naturally, and there had been both laughter and tears. It did not fully dispel the inner unsettling sense that something was wrong for any of us, but it did take it down several notches.

The Aftermath

A week later, when I thought things had returned to normal, I went to lunch with a friend I had gotten to know after Jack died. She asked how he'd died, and I was right back in the moments of his death. Words poured out of me like a flood from a fire hose and could not be stopped. Every bit of it was real. All of the trauma overwhelmed me: the house filled with police and ambulance crews, not being allowed in the ambulance, the waiting at the hospital, the endless time it took before I was allowed back into his room, the way I was treated as a suspect until I agreed to an autopsy, not being able to be with him as he was dying. The details just came out as I relived them as a vivid experience with all five senses. My friend quietly met my eyes through the telling and shed a few tears, making space for me to shed my tears. What became clear was that I was doing all right with grief and loss, but not with the trauma surrounding the event.

It was like being in a state of shock, and it lasted for a couple of days. I was shaky, disoriented, and there were loops of negative commentary playing in my head and undermining my confidence and ability to move in the world. It took weeks to tie this to my strong sense that I had failed the person I loved by not being able to prevent the repetition of prolonged useless medical treatment. I had tried to follow his deep wish to donate organs but failed. Part of who I believe I am is the person you can count on, but when it came to these most personal and profound promises, no matter how I tried, I could not deliver.

During those weeks, I felt that anyone who spoke with me must see that something was wrong. I found myself telling individuals what was going on, in part so they would not take personally what I felt was strange or distant behavior. Telling helped dissipate the sense of being dissociated from the life going on around me, and it helped my son and daughter, who were suffering with similar issues. It was as if we had separated Jack's death from the trauma surrounding it and were now finally putting it together. Telling a friend, when I knew that I could have gotten away with hiding what was wrong, deepened the friendship and made me feel a little safer in the world. Trying to be strong, trying to just engage with new life did not work. Letting others into the struggle did.

It was tough to make the choice to have these conversations. I had accepted an unacknowledged expectation that after two years, you should move on. Intellectually, I did not believe this; other, bigger parts of me did. A hidden part of me felt that if I was perceived to be a burden for too long, I would end up alone in the world. I feared that visible, ongoing struggle would frighten others away. I wished our rituals and our plans to honor significant dates could contain my grief. But they were not enough. The path toward a full life seems to demand integration of loss with living and an honesty that sometimes strips me bare.

Thoughts

♦ **Your inner calendar knows a milestone is coming.**

♦ **Telling stories helps.**

♦ **Loss, especially sudden loss, creates trauma as well as grief.**

♦ **Regrets carry a lot of weight.**

♦ **Grief is grief, yet we each have our own brand.**

♦ **Anger at death and at grief is part of the deal.**

♦ **Letting others into the struggle can help.**

Making Sense of Now

When I began this book, my focus was on those days that carry special meaning, the days that knock us to our knees, exhaust us to think about, and demand a creative response. When the phrase "milestone days" occurred to me, I did not realize that these days really were milestones or rites of passage for me. Looking back, I can see that each time I chose to consciously acknowledge and live the pain and potential of a milestone day, I moved along the path of an emerging strength and self.

These days brought into sharp focus the balance of mourning and living, retreat and engagement, self-care and service.

The difficult days brought me time and again to the process of discovering how being loved and loving in the safety of a marriage had changed me. They gave me reasons to find my strength, connect to the self who is surfacing, and find new ways to connect with the world around me. As regular reminders of the fragility of life, they nudged me to live the life I have with any courage and imagination I can muster.

Learning how to cope with holidays turns out to have changed how I manage so many of the ordinary places and times when grief comes unbidden. For at least the first year after Jack died, taking out the garbage or making a small home repair was emotionally charged, and sometimes still is. Maintaining the gardens around our house brings up what to keep and what to make my own. Going to a graduation, wedding, or a grandchild's birthday party challenges my ability to balance the wish to celebrate and the sense that I alone am not enough.

Each time, I feel an acute desire to share the experience with my partner, who would have taken great delight in attending. Disclosing instead of hiding this desire seems to be opening me more deeply to sharing in the joy and love of the people who are there to celebrate.

Grief and the challenges it brings changed me. Facing the fear of getting lost in emptiness taught me about embracing life. Feeling the pain taught me about planning space for it and forced me to learn how to grieve with others. Watching how grief diminished my capacity taught me compassion and gave me understanding that lets me initiate difficult conversations and listen with an open heart.

As you may have noticed in my story, grief becomes easier to manage over time. Bouts of acute pain or times when grief hijacks me are decreasing. I can't imagine a time when my family and I will want to stop acknowledging Jack and our gratitude for his presence in our lives. But we have found some new traditions and ways to continue old traditions that work. We are getting pretty good at weaving our mourning into both milestone days and the times when it just comes up naturally.

Most of the time now, my heart smiles when the guy who looks just like Jack rides his bicycle past the house, wearing a jacket that matches the one Jack wore when he rode his bicycle home to me.

Part Two

Others'
Journeys

Chapter Six

Stories and Ideas from Others' Experiences

In the process of grieving and healing, I've come to know a number of folks who've traveled their own paths through love, loss, and coming back to life. In this next section, I'll briefly share some strategies and ideas they have shared. Additional suggestions are listed in the Appendix.

Success Is a Decision

I'll begin with a story of a man who was mourning the death of his childhood sweetheart, wife of forty-eight years, and business partner.

Paul

Paul's wife was his whole life for fifty years. When she died, he just shut down. Paul's family follows the Jewish tradition of sitting Shiva. After a death, the first-degree relatives gather in one home for several days. They can sit quietly, share stories, or talk with other mourners who stop by to pay their respects. Paul didn't want to sit Shiva or talk about feelings or himself. His grief felt profoundly private.

Paul said that with his wife's death and the disappearance of her smile, all his vibrancy and love of life felt extinguished. He described himself as simply vegetating for fifty to sixty days, then trying to find solace in work. On their anniversary, he just sat in a chair and moped. At Hanukah, he shared the gifts his wife had purchased and wrapped, but his focus was inward and protective of his feelings. Milestone days were just days with extra pain.

During these first months, friends and family phoned daily to check in, but he only felt comfortable talking about non-personal things. He fought feeling good, because his wife was not there to share the experience. He described a sense that he did not have the right to be enjoying life if his wife could not. It was like walking in a desert with no direction, no paths, just dangling.

After three months, Paul sensed that things were getting very bad. He would just work and sleep, and in his chosen isolation, ignore gentle pushes from family to join in things. At this point, he said, "To hell with this, I am going to stand on my own two feet. I have to fix this." Using an approach that worked in his business, he asserted, "Success is a decision. I will work myself out of this thing. I'll do one positive thing every day."

Paul described this as a major turning point that changed his life. He found strength to live into this decision by going to the cemetery and sharing his thoughts with his wife. For a long time, he took these steps mechanically, because he felt he should, not for the joy of it. One of Paul's choices was to find a way to use his own talents, energy, and intelligence to become a volunteer. It gave him something to do. He began working out again, saw a grief counselor, and started talking to other widowers at a bereavement group. There was great relief in the safe haven of a group of nonjudgmental people who would listen without lecturing.

Five months after his wife's death, Paul made a second decision: to reconnect with his daughters and their families. His wife had been the one who was the glue in family cele-brations and relationships. Without her, he felt a keen sense of isolation and the need for the serious conversations he had avoided by always keeping busy. He was afraid that he and his family didn't know one another anymore. He had been keep-ing his daughters at arm's length and decided it was time to change, so he requested an adult family gathering.

Paul's plan was to begin to get to know his children as adults, to create a time to talk about more than what the grandkids were doing. His family agreed to his request and things have been changing. He reached out to a granddaughter, and they have become close. She is a gentle help to him in family events he would have attended with his wife. He continues to speak with his wife regularly, but now he takes walks for these conversations.

Thoughts

♦ **Positive steps, even if they are small, can accumulate.**

♦ **Bereavement groups can be a powerful part of healing.**

♦ **Family relationships can grow and change after a loss.**

Paul doesn't know if there will come a time when he doesn't feel as if there is a cloud over his head, stifling joy, exhilaration, and laughter. But there are increasing glimmers of sunlight. When he feels he has hit a block, he returns to his plan to do one positive thing each day and to reconnect with his family.

Keeping Things the Same

A number of widows and widowers I've met have found comfort and strength in sticking closely to traditions, keeping things as much the same as possible. Here are a couple of those stories.

Ingrid

Ingrid's wish is to do the holidays the same way as they have been done in her home for as long as she can manage. The things that need to be reinvented—how to manage her husband, Frank's, birthday or their anniversary—are what make her frightened and sad. She prefers to struggle through these days on her own.

On traditional holidays such as Thanksgiving and Christmas, comfort comes from the familiar routines. She says, "My German heritage leads me to do what is in front of me." Doing things the way they have always been done lets Ingrid avoid the effort of planning something new and negotiating conflicting advice from children and stepchildren.

Hosting the familiar holiday gatherings is both a challenge and a pleasure for Ingrid. She said, "My life feels like a deck of cards that someone has tossed into the air. No matter how hard I try to gather them, they just keep slipping away. The feeling is at its worst during family get-togethers. I never truly appreciated how much my husband contributed to our celebrations."

Many practical concerns arise when tasks that were shared are no longer shared, or when knowledge Frank possessed, like how to work the coffeepot, is gone. There are personal concerns as well. Ingrid finds herself hoping the grandchildren will have a good time and want to come back, struggling to become clear-headed enough to ask for help, and learning to relax into holidays when things may not go as well as expected.

Getting things ready for holidays takes longer now, but the burden lifts when family arrives. Somehow, things get done, and when the unexpected happens, it is most often a source of humor. There will be some comments about Frank being missing, but the days are pleasant. The family has conversations about Frank that may lead to tears, but they are shared tears.

Despite the struggles, Ingrid finds great satisfaction in being able to continue important traditions. She feels that they are sorting out the logistics of the holidays as a family. It brings her joy to see her family connect and form new ways of keeping the traditions.

Thoughts

♦ **Keeping things the same can be comforting.**

♦ **Letting go of the expectation that you can do it all perfectly leaves room for humor, sharing the load, and new connections.**

Allen

Allen's wife, Susan, died in September, less than three months before Christmas. Her health had declined during a thirteen-year illness, but her death was unexpected. Allen and his two adult children did not decorate their homes that first Christmas. It was too difficult to think about being happy. Allen was hesitant about how to celebrate and did not know how it would be. A small family group spent the day together and spoke with extended family by phone.

For the first Christmas after Susan's death, Allen made books for family members. He created individual hardcover books for himself and his children. Each book had photos and prose or poems that would have special meaning to the recipient. For Susan's siblings, Allen made individual softcover books.

He also made calendars for everyone, with photos and all of the important dates and phone numbers in Susan's family. The calendars are a way to help the kids stay connected to their mother's relatives. Allen pulls the calendar out whenever he gets the feeling that there is a date he is forgetting. Both the calendars and the books are a source of comfort.

Allen said they were technically easy and inexpensive to create. But, he continued, "They were emotionally difficult to do. Making the books was good therapy. I got to think about Susan as who she was to me and who she was to others. It helped to engage with the photos from special times in her life with the family."

Allen also made a slide presentation of all of the photos from the books and calendars and gave a copy to each family member.

Allen puts the most emphasis on St. Patrick's Day and December 30, Susan's birthday. These holidays were important to Susan, and her passion made them the most important to him. He is not good with dates, so his kids will remind him of upcoming anniversaries or other key days by calling to ask what he will be doing on that day. Allen feels that the kids need something to happen more than he does. But it helps them all to get together. They usually come to his home for dinner just to be together and share stories.

St. Patrick's Day was a big day for Susan and their adopted daughter, because they shared an Irish heritage. First thing in the morning, Allen calls his daughter to wake her and wish her a Happy St. Patrick's Day. The day before, he goes out and gets decorations and Irish-themed gifts for his daughter to wear. The family will have dinner together, and it will be whatever the kids want. When Susan was alive, they ate corned beef and cabbage, because she loved it. But they do not feel the need to keep the meal the same. It is enough to eat together.

Susan's birthday is also celebrated at home. In the past, there were some grand celebrations, and they enjoy reminiscing about them and Susan's terrific smile and laugh. The birthdays are markers of how her loveliness remained through all of the changes her health problems brought. Having dinner at home now keeps the expenses down, and the privacy of the house allows them to talk more comfortably. They share their different personal memories, and Allen brings out photos as part of the event. The dinners feel easy and have a natural flow.

Ever since that first Christmas, Allen's family has settled into a comfortable tradition of celebrating most of the important dates and holidays by sharing small gifts and a meal. They feel it would have made Susan feel bad if they did not do this. Their celebrations are similar to the ones in the years prior to Susan's death. Since Susan was ill for thirteen years, their celebrations had become small and primarily with family. Before she became ill, parties may have included up to 150 people. But as her health declined, going out was not a pleasure that she enjoyed, and crowds became a problem, so they shaped their events around Susan's changing needs.

Allen said, "In my deep love for Susan, even if it is something I would not normally do, I will probably observe birthdays and other special days in ways she would have."

Many times when they get together as a family, they share stories that are based on Susan. Their grief continues, but it helps his children tremendously to discuss some of the memories. Having dinner at Allen's home is part of creating tradition that acknowledges loss and makes it okay to feel sad and miss their mom.

Thoughts

♦ **Making gifts that share memories can be therapeutic.**

♦ **Sometimes it is enough to be together at home, where privacy gives you the space to share stories.**

♦ **Observing the milestones that were important to your loved one is an expression of your love.**

Balancing Keeping the Traditions the Same while Adding New Elements
Rachel

Rachel spoke about sharing a love of travel with her husband, Bernie, and the travel she has done since he died. Thanksgiving occurred about six weeks after his death. Sitting Shiva at the time of Bernie's death gave the family time to talk and plan for Thanksgiving. They agreed to spend the holiday with the same people in much the same way but in a different venue. Rachel and other family members traveled to a relative's home in a city her husband loved. Rachel felt that if they celebrated in the same location, the sense of the seat that was empty would have been too sharp.

For his birthday, she traveled to visit with family in California, where they shared a dinner in his memory and chatted about him. Rachel was invited to the Passover Seder she and Bernie had regularly attended. She went and was glad that she did.

Rachel said, "Making new traditions helps change my feelings." She struggles to feel comfortable alone at gatherings that she and Bernie used to attend together, so she is trying to balance those events with new activities. On the day of the month that Bernie died, she feels a need to honor him in some way. She finds herself noticing the date and thinking about what transpired on that day.

Before Bernie became too ill, they had regularly hosted a Hanukah party for friends and family. The second Hanukah after his death, she invited friends who were comfortable mentioning Bernie and talking about the things he liked.

One of the rich aspects of Rachel and Bernie's life was going out often for dinner or to shows or to be with friends. For her wedding anniversary in April, she went out to a park with her son in the afternoon. In the evening, she went with her sister to dinner and a play. The quality of the production and engagement in a good drama took her out of her own life and was a welcome respite from thinking about loss.

Bernie was an avid genealogist. After becoming ill, he began and completed an account of the family's history in Poland.

As part of his investigation, he traveled to Argentina, England, Poland, and Israel. Genealogy helped him make peace with losing his professional life to illness, and it brought him new relationships that his family continues. To honor Bernie's legacy and to pay tribute to his memory, eight family members have planned a trip to Poland. For part of the trip, they will travel with Bernie's private guide and census translator. They will visit the places Bernie found and visited and also some places in Eastern Europe that will be new to all of them.

Advice from Two Widows

A couple of widows I spoke with talked about renewing traditions that had become impossible as their spouses' health had declined. Each of them traveled to celebrations with extended family. They found comfort and satisfaction in rejoining the larger group.

Thoughts

♦ **Find a way to soften the acute pain of your loss on milestone days.**

♦ **Include people who are comfortable talking about your loved one.**

♦ **Is there an activity you can plan that will honor your loved one's legacy?**

♦ **Are there traditions you lost during an extended illness that you can reclaim?**

The Elephant in the Room

A number of people I interviewed described very unsatisfying attempts to deal with milestone days. The common theme was feeling that their spouses' absence seemed to be the elephant in the room. Some of these attempts were arrangements to be with a friend or friends on an anniversary or birthday. Others were more celebratory events such as attending a Father's Day party. They described a deep wish to chat about their spouse or to have someone ask how they were doing. It never seemed to be clear whether others were actively avoiding the topic, being cautious about letting the bereaved spouse start the conversation, or just that they had moved on to thinking about other things.

Thoughts

♦ **Some people cannot grieve with you.**

♦ **Opening the door to those who can is essential.**

♦ **Time alone is also essential.**

There was no consensus about how to effectively handle this, but there was agreement that some friends and family are much better at grieving with you than are others; some just need you to open the door, and some simply cannot go there. There was also agreement that sometimes you are ready to open the door and share, and sometimes you just need to be alone.

Chapter Seven

Formal Acts
of Remembrance

Two Ash-Scattering Ceremonies
Allen

Allen's wife had donated her body to science, so he received Susan's ashes in the fall, about a year after she died. Since the family always had Thanksgiving in Maine, and Susan always enjoyed being in Maine, Allen decided to have the ceremony there over the Thanksgiving holiday. He notified family members so that they could join him if they wished. Many did. He arranged for family to meet at a bed-and-breakfast, and extended family from both sides stayed for three days.

Allen designed the ash-scattering ceremony using ideas from his children, prayers, and songs to sing and listen to from his wedding to Susan. As background music, he used the same CD he had compiled for her memorial service. He made a program for the ceremony with readings and photos of Susan. It included the Irish Blessing: "And until we meet again, May God hold you in the palm of his hand." He led the ceremony he had designed.

Both of Allen's children and his brother-in-law asked ahead of time if they could keep some of her ashes. Allen found some Irish china that was decorated with a segment of the Irish saying used in the program. He put some of the ashes in each of those containers and sealed them with super glue. Most of the ashes were passed around at the ceremony, then scattered in the ocean.

Some family members wanted to have a small part of the ashes to scatter quietly, privately, so Allen had prepared containers for them. Susan and Allen had not wanted to take up space on the earth with their bodies after their death. But he said, "We had not thought about how difficult it would be for the kids not to have a gravestone." So he planned to put up a stone in front of Susan's parents' stone. That way, there will be a place, but it will not take up any additional space.

Over the course of the year before this service, Allen gathered items Susan had kept that were special to her because someone special had given them to her. On the weekend of the ash-scattering ceremony, he gave back things that he felt people would treasure. An example was letters from an older brother when he was in Vietnam.

Catherine

Catherine's family performed a simpler ash-scattering ceremony. Most of the family lived locally, so they picked a date on which the few who needed to travel could come. They gathered at an isolated spot along a lake, where they shared memories of their loved one and a prayer from their Buddhist tradition. A family member who had brought flowers passed them out to the group. The oldest son scattered all of the ashes into the water, and, one by one, the rest of the family tossed their flowers into the water. They reported that watching the ashes float away brought a sense of letting go. The flowers trailing the ashes floating out toward the center of the lake made a beautiful and peaceful sight.

A Headstone Unveiling

Rachel spoke about the comfort and simplicity in planning to use a traditional ceremony for the ritual of unveiling the headstone one year after a death. Using the structure and prayers of a well-established service fit with her family's interest in their history and accommodated Rachel's wish not to have to create a ceremony. Rachel's daughter Sarah wanted all of the traditional things to be on her dad's headstone and did the research. They were able to order the stone to match a grandparent's stone. A friend did the research to find an appropriate service, one with traditional structure and prayers, that had space for the adult children to be actively involved.

Two Tributes
Larry

Three months after his wife, Julie, died, Larry had an unexpected opportunity to pay tribute to his wife's memory with family. He traveled to Ohio to honor Julie's wishes that he attend her niece's wedding. He wanted to show his face and be with Julie's family. He went out a few days ahead and stayed with a couple of Julie's sisters. Staying with both of them was nice, and they had time to share some memories.

Thoughts

♦ **Different grievers may have different needs at rituals.**

♦ **Think about finding a place that will allow you all to grieve as you scatter ashes.**

♦ **People may treasure the return of gifts they gave to the deceased.**

♦ **Your religious tradition may provide a ceremony that works for you.**

While he was in Ohio, he learned from his sister-in-law that the funeral home had not sent an announcement to Julie's hometown newspaper. The family decided that writing an "In Memoriam" for Julie would be the right thing. As Larry said, "Better late than never." With input from extended family members, Larry created a piece for the local paper. He included Julie's repeated message to him, "I've lived a very good life and am not afraid to die." Larry found he felt better after sharing Julie's words and creating recognition for her in her hometown.

Jeanne

Jeanne created her own ceremony to mark the anniversary of her husband's death. She gathered wildflowers, supplemented them with some purchased cut flowers, and made a large, loosely tied bouquet. She brought grandchildren with her to a pier on a lake where they tied the bouquet to a post. She took pictures of the children and the bouquet, then they slowly released the flowers one by one into the water. Jeanne's spouse had suffered with a long, painful illness. In her heart, she felt an emerging peace, as if she were releasing him from his pain and suffering. She sent photos of the event to all family members who had not been present.

Thoughts

♦ **Tributes can be made when you feel the urge to create them.**

♦ **A satisfying ceremony can be very simple.**

Chapter Eight

Conclusion

Grief is exhausting. It can drive us to our knees, overtake us suddenly, and challenge us over and over again to find ways to simultaneously live and mourn. The milestone days bring added struggles. They demand creativity from us when grief is at its most overwhelming and befuddling. Perhaps you recognize the feelings of diminished capacity, unmooring, and fear of getting lost in grief that you found in these stories. I hope that you also found some comfort and some ideas that may support you in your mourning process and your search for ways to both honor your loss and live into the present.

Appendix

This book and the healing process of writing it emerged from conversations: conversations with myself, with books as I read them, with family, friends, and other grievers. I saw that even though our upbringing, family structures, loss experiences, and faiths differed, there was some common core of grief that transcended our differences. This book is an extension of these conversations to include you. If you feel a pull to continue the conversation and perhaps share some of your own experiences, please consider joining the discussion at www.mourningandmilestones.com.

The next section contains two lists that grew from the conversations that inspired this book. First is a set of questions I learned to ask myself before an approaching birthday, holiday, anniversary, or other milestone. Next are suggestions for ways to honor your loved one's life. Finally, I've included our ash-scattering ceremony as a sample of a structure that worked. I hope that these ideas provide a useful starting place as you and your loved ones face your own milestones.

Questions to Ask
as a Milestone Approaches

- What do I need on this day?
  - ○ Am I feeling particularly vulnerable?
  - ○ Do I need to be alone?
  - ○ Is this a day to be with others?
  - ○ Is there a balance of both that works?
  - ○ Am I leaving enough space for the unexpected to arise?
- How much planning do I want to do?
- How far ahead do I need to plan?
- Can I get away with ignoring this one, or will it bite me anyway?
- Is there a good distraction that might help?
- Do I need space to see how the day will evolve?
- Do I want to make this a day of remembrance, a day of new focus, or both?
- Do I want to make a small gesture of remembrance?
- Who might be able to help?
  - ○ Who would be good company?
  - ○ Whom do I feel safe being around when I am vulnerable?
  - ○ Whom might I want to not include?
  - ○ Do I want to be with someone who will talk with me about my loved one or someone who will focus more on the activity of the day—or one of each?

- If it is a major milestone or holiday:
  - What tasks are truly necessary?
  - What tasks can be shared or off-loaded?
  - Who can help with keeping the important traditions?
  - What can change about how we celebrate?
    - Venue
    - Food
    - Activity
    - People
  - What do I want/need to keep the same?
  - Will I need some alone time?
  - What will I do if no one mentions my loved one?
    - Do I want them mentioned?
    - Is there a socially comfortable way I can bring them up?
    - Do I need to ask anyone ahead of time for support with this issue?
  - What if I lose it?

Some Suggestions That Can Be Used for Any Day of Remembrance

Many people mentioned finding ways to incorporate the qualities you loved in your loved one into your own life or in a memorial as a way of answering the question "How do they live on?" Here are some ideas.

- Donate to a cause or keep up a membership they valued.

- Volunteer for a cause they cared about.

- Create physical reminders to the world of their life and passions.

   o Donate to a library for purchase of a book in their name. The library purchases the book and puts a bookplate inside naming the honoree.

   o Donate to a favorite park for a bench with a plaque naming the honoree.

   o Donate to a botanical garden or park to plant a tree or perennial bed in their honor.

   o Fund a city vegetable garden.

   o Form a scholarship fund in their name.

   o Cook their favorite food.

- Make a deeper effort to connect to children or grandchildren.

- Focus on a quality—such as generosity, fairness, compassion, curiosity, or other trait—that you valued and try to nurture this in yourself.

- Take a trip to a place they loved.

Adding New Elements to Traditions: Ways to Honor Your Loved One on Milestone Days

- Light a candle each morning of the holiday season and let it burn all day as a symbol of your loved one's presence.

- Choose things from their belongings and give them as gifts to those who loved him or her.

- Buy your loved one a gift and donate it.

- Buy an ornament for your Christmas tree.

- Plant something.

- Toast your loved one at a holiday meal.

- Read aloud one of your loved one's favorite poems or passages.

- Read aloud a letter your loved one wrote.

- Share photos on social media.

- Share photos around the table.

- Play a piece of your loved one's favorite music.

- Bring branches from the Christmas tree to the cemetery and lay them on the grave.

- Place flowers or a wreath at the cemetery.

- Use the day as a day of service: visit a nursing home, serve meals at a food kitchen, or perform a service that held meaning for you both.

- On gift-giving holidays, frame a photo for each family member or attendee of that person with your loved one.

Our Ash-Scattering Ceremony

This sample ash-scattering ceremony is the one that we used to memorialize my husband, Jack. Please feel free to use this as a base when planning your own ceremony and add or remove whatever feels right to honor your loved one.

1) Introduction

We've gathered to honor our husband, father, uncle, and grandfather's wish to have his ashes scattered in the beauty of the Algonquin. As he said in his letter to us, it was a place that was important to him as a boy, as a father, as a grandfather, and as a husband. Together, we bring his remains to the place he chose to return to. As we join to complete this task that we all hoped would not be part of our lives for many years to come, our collective presence honors each of our unique connections and relationships to Jack/Dad/Poppa/Uncle and his love for each and all of us. I know that our joys are greater, our ability to love is deeper, and our lives are richer because we shared his life. For me, this is a time both to shed tears that he is gone and to smile because he lived.

Let us begin with a prayer that reflects Jack's choice to have us gather in the wilderness as we say good-bye.

O God, in the course of this busy life, give us times of refreshment and peace; and grant that we may so use our leisure to rebuild our bodies and renew our minds, that our spirits may be opened to the goodness of your creation; through Jesus Christ our Lord. Amen.

2) Reading

A reading in honor of the life of Lawrence Jackson Fraser.

To laugh often and much; to win the respect of intelligent people and the affection of children; to earn the appre-

ciation of honest critics; and endure the betrayal of false friends; to appreciate beauty; to find the best in others; to leave the world a bit better, whether by a healthy child, a garden patch, or a redeemed social condition; to know that one life has breathed easier because you lived here. This is to have succeeded.

—Ralph Waldo Emerson

3) Song

A song as we hold Lawrence Jackson Fraser in our hearts. (NOTE: You can sing the songs you choose, or have a player handy to simply let everyone listen quietly or sing along.) We chose the song "Carry" by Tori Amos.

4) Time for reflections, silent and spoken.

5) Messages to Friends/Family from the Loved One

A message to my grandchildren.

If ever there is a tomorrow when we're not together, there is something you must always remember. You are braver than you believe, stronger than you seem, and smarter than you think. But the most important thing is even if we are apart, I'll always be with you.

—A. A. Milne

6) A Time to Scatter Ashes and a Verse to Sing

May the long time sun shine
   upon you

Thoughts

♦ **The structure you create in your ritual will provide a sense of safety.**

♦ **Think about including both readings and music.**

♦ **Offer participants a chance to lead music or read part of the ceremony.**

♦ **Include an opening, a closing, and a chance for everyone to speak.**

All love surround you
And the pure light within you
Guide your way home

7) Closing

A prayer as we move back into the world.

Lord, make us instruments of your peace. Where there is hatred, let us sow love; where there is injury, pardon; where there is discord, union; where there is doubt, faith; where there is despair, hope; where there is darkness, light; where there is sadness, joy. Grant that we may not so much seek to be consoled as to console; to be understood as to understand; to be loved as to love. For it is in giving that we receive; it is in pardoning that we are pardoned; and it is in dying that we are born to eternal life. Amen.

—(attributed to) St. Francis